# COLLEGE
# ADMISSION

Copyright © 2019 by NSHSS

**College Admission: How to Get Into Your Dream School—Real Students, Real Stories**

All rights reserved. No part of this publication may be reproduced, distributed, or transmitted in any form or by any means, including photocopying, recording, or other electronic or mechanical methods, without the prior written permission of the publisher, except in the case of brief quotations embodied in reviews and certain other non-commercial uses permitted by copyright law.

Printed in the United States of America

First Printing, 2019

ISBN 978-0-9980362-0-5

National Society of High School Scholars
1936 North Druid Hills Rd NE
Atlanta, GA 30319

www.StudentSuccessStories.com

# COLLEGE ADMISSION

## ADMISSION

How to Get Into Your Dream School

## REAL STUDENTS,
### REAL STORIES

*TO MY PARENTS*
*for raising me to believe that*
*anything is possible*

And

*TO MY WIFE, LEE*
*for her unconditional love and support*

And

*TO MY CHILDREN:*
*AUSTIN, ANNIE, AND HUDSON*
*for the inspiration they have given me*
*as they achieved their own dreams*

And

*TO MY GRANDCHILDREN:*
*NOAH, JACOB, AND BABY JAMES*
*for the love and joy that*
*they bring to all of our lives*

# COLLEGE ADMISSION
## HOW TO GET INTO YOUR DREAM SCHOOL

# REAL STUDENTS,
## REAL STORIES

# THE "DREAM SCHOOLS"

Agnes Scott College

American Musical Dramatic Academy

American University

Austin College

Bard College at Simon's Rock

Barnard College

Baylor University

Bowling Green State University

Brown University

Carleton University

Carnegie Mellon University

Cornell University

Dartmouth College

Drexel University

Eastern Michigan University

Fashion Institute of Design and
Merchandising

Florida Institute of Technology

Florida State University

Georgia Institute of Technology

Georgetown University

Hampton University

Laguna College of Art and Design

Lehigh University

Nebraska Wesleyan

New York University

North Carolina State University

Oglethorpe University

Ringling College of Art and Design

Spelman College

The Ohio State University

The University of Texas at Austin

United States Naval Academy

University of Akron

University of California, Berkeley

University of California, Los Angeles

University of Chicago

University of Florida

University of Southern California

Wellesley College

Yale University

*Students and tourists around the world rub John Harvard's shoe for good luck.*

# Foreword

James Lewis's book "College Admission: Real Students, Real Stories" about current students and their experiences in high school and during the college admissions process is a wonderful and important addition to helpful resources at a time that too often is filled with angst. As one who has been an educator for 45 years, including the last 27 as a college counselor, I found the book to be uniquely layered with both peer-to-peer and professional advice that could make a significant difference for applicants and their parents. As Lewis and those whose stories are told demonstrate, a student's dream school can be well known or a hidden gem, and it is important for all families to keep an open mind about which schools may truly be "best fits" in preparing students for careers and meaningful lives.

Nancy T. Beane
Associate Director of College Counseling at
The Westminster Schools in Atlanta, GA
Former President of the National Association
for College Admission Counseling

# A Letter from Claes Nobel

*Senior member of the family that established the Nobel Prizes*

DEAR STUDENTS,

I truly believe that you are the future of our world, the future leaders. Each and every one of you is capable of achieving greatness both in your personal and professional life. You should be proud of your hard work and what you have achieved so far, but you cannot allow yourself to become complacent. This is the time for you to seek opportunities to learn, to grow, and to expand your mind, so you can reach your full human potential. You do not need to wait for the future to start making your mark on the world. Achieving greatness takes time, so you must begin now to take steps to accomplish your goals. This is your moment; RIGHT NOW, seize it, and begin on your path towards future success. This is your moment to: "Be More!"

This book, "College Admission: How to Get into Your Dream School—Real Students, Real Stories," was created to help you be your best. The idea of recognizing the best has been the goal of the Swedish Nobel family for nearly 120 years. My great-grand uncle, Dr. Alfred Nobel, started a mission of Peace & Excellence for World Betterment by establishing The Nobel Prize. While it is an honor and a privilege to recognize the greatest scientists, poets, statesmen, and philosophers among us, there is a special place in my heart for encouraging, recognizing, and empowering the young people of the world.

I encourage you to form unique friendships and build a lasting network now that helps you and your peers advance in the future. Use the gifts and talents you have been given, leverage your academic achievements earned, and you will be empowered to change the world to make it better, safer, and saner.

I know that as young scholars, you are deeply passionate not only about academics, but also about the conditions of your community and the world. Today, we live in a time when differences often dominate our dialogue. When you young, emerging leaders are given respect, support, validation, and encouragement, you then have the power to make profound and lasting changes to our society.

Serving as Co-founder and Chairman of the National Society of High School Scholars, an organization dedicated to honoring and empowering youth worldwide, I am continuously inspired by the unquenchable spirit of young students. You and your peers represent the best and brightest minds of the Millennial Generation and Generation-Z. The stories in this book illustrate that those among you not only succeed academically, but also are actively involved in community service and civic engagement, and have already begun to leave your mark on the world.

This book is filled with advice from a diverse network of students, industry experts, and universities. Together, we hope to support you as you continue your education, pursue meaningful career opportunities, and lead lives of true purpose.

To the parents of our readers: Thank you for supporting your wonderful children as they set out to accomplish their goals. We thank you, your children thank you, and the world thanks you. There is wise advice for you in this book as well.

Young scholars, I have enormous faith in each and every one of you. You have within you the power to achieve your goals and make a positive impact on the world. Acceptance to the college of your dreams is an important step toward your own personal greatness. Be Honored by what you have already achieved...and then go forward to Be More.

Good Earth!

Claes Nobel

# Introduction

If getting into college is an important goal in your life, then you can likely relate to the sentiments of Esther M. Bedoyan, a student at Carnegie Mellon University: "At the start of my freshman year in high school, the prospect of attending college seemed abstract and distant. The application process seemed like a long and harrowing ordeal that would either result in success or failure." Despite her original misgivings, this student landed at a top-notch university to study biomedical engineering. She adds, "Reflecting upon my college application process from its start to finish, I now realize that it was simultaneously draining and exhilarating, and it helped me learn more about myself and allowed me to build self-confidence. Ultimately, through a lot of hard work, persistence, and the help of my family, school counselors, teachers and friends, I was able to achieve my goal of identifying and getting accepted into the college that best suits my career goals and holistic interests—my dream school, Carnegie Mellon University."

Esther's observations perfectly sum up what this book is about. *College Admission: How to Get Into Your Dream School—Real Students, Real Stories* is a how-to guide for college-bound students and their families filled with personal, relevant guidance and useful information in the college search and application process. Students who have successfully joined the ranks of their dream schools share their own journeys and first-hand experiences that led them to college acceptance. The real stories and essay samples from real students pursuing a wide range of school options—from community colleges to the Ivy League—set this book apart as a relatable and rich resource for anyone looking to find your best-fit college or university.

More than anything, I want the pages that follow to help you clarify your own hopes and dreams as you pursue a college education. I'm reminded of a wise saying:

> "The two most important days of your life are the day you are born and the day you find out why."

For many, the college application process and college itself are the important steps that reveal your true purpose in life. I believe that the lifelong pursuit of education is critical to helping us all discover who we are and what our purpose is in life.

My passion and life's work has been to focus on opening doors of opportunity for all young people—of all races, creeds, colors, and income levels. Having access to a good education is critical to a person's development, and I strive for equal access for everyone. To that end, I've spent the last 40 years visiting college campuses and meeting with admissions officers and representatives at more than 150 institutions across the U.S.

Through my experiences of working with more than a million students at the National Society of High School Scholars (NSHSS), a student organization co-founded with Mr. Claes Nobel, I have been able to comfort and guide students and families through the college admission process, which is often overwrought with anxiety, competition, worry, and fear. The majority of students in high school (a full 70% in my estimation) do not yet have a strong sense of self. Most of you are still going through that process of identifying who you are, who you may want to become, what you want to study, where you want to go, and how you will pay for it. The uncertainty is difficult for families. It's a challenge because we know the importance of a good education and its capacity to elevate you, your family, and your future family. We know how access to a college can be a profoundly important step in life and is one of the most critical factors for personal and professional happiness (however you define happiness). The stakes are high.

My motivation for writing ***College Admission: How to Get Into Your Dream School—Real Students, Real Stories*** was to provide guidance to all students, including first-generation college applicants, parents, and family members. I want to reassure you that no matter where you are on the path to college, it's OK. My dream is to enable all students to have an equal shot at going to a great school—equal footing for hope. You can dream big, explore multiple educational opportunities, discover who you are and what you want to be along the way. It is OK if you don't know what you want to study, where you want to go, and how you're going to get there yet. Really...it's OK.

The journey we all go through in life is full of surprises and ups and downs. As a student, you will experience those ups and downs vividly during high school and as you navigate the college application process. NSHSS sponsored a scholarship competition inviting students to share their personal stories of how they got into their dream schools. The flood of responses revealed the hard work, perseverance, and sheer wisdom of students who have been through the process. We were inspired by their first-hand experiences and decided to collect some of the best tips and most authentic stories to share in this book. You will hear of high school students' dreams about taking that next step, exploring different options, coming up with cool solutions to defining their dream school, and building on the foundation for their future dreams and their lives.

These stories are an important testimony to the challenges students have had to overcome and the decisions they have had to make along the way. The information is for all families. I hope the book will motivate students, parents, and siblings to start thinking early about college and to better understand how you define your dream college experience. We share stories of students who changed their minds—sometimes at the last possible moment—about what their dream school is and what area of study they want to pursue.

These words from real students who have "been there and done that" tell the real story and hold weight in my book—in any book. Much of the advice and personal insight into the college application process that our students offer is applicable to anyone. These life lessons or pearls of wisdom, as one of our scholarship winners calls them, will serve you well through high school, college, and beyond.

*James W. Lewis*

# What is a Dream School, Anyway?

Everyone's dream is different. And there is a dream school out there for everyone.

*First and foremost, a dream college doesn't have to be what you initially thought you wanted. There are a number of unforeseen factors that come into play when selecting a college that one may not have considered early on in the process. What constitutes the perfect college for each person differs, but the journey is more or less similar for us all, which makes it helpful to learn through the experiences of others.*

—Abbigal Maeng, Austin College

If you base your ideal on reputation and competitiveness alone, the Ivy League schools come up first on that list. These eight elite institutions include Brown University, Columbia University, Cornell University, Dartmouth College, Harvard University, Princeton University, University of Pennsylvania, and Yale University. Known for academic excellence, these schools have their pick of the best students and athletes in the world. Lots of students dream of attending an Ivy, but only 5% to 10% of those who apply are accepted. It's important to remember that even some of the brightest students do not get accepted to these top universities. Although these schools are considered "top universities" they are not the right fit for even some of the very best students. And if you are a cream-of-the-crop student, you may have other schools on your "dream" list. Location (other than the cold northeast, for example), size (smaller or larger than the 4,000 to 20,000 students at these eight schools), academic focus, or financial considerations can open up a whole range of other school options that fit your ideal.

*Throughout my entire research process of looking for undergraduate and graduate programs, I was not focused on applying to Ivy League schools, nor did I even look at any of the programs offered at Ivy League schools. Yes, Ivy League schools may seem better to some people, but the purpose of college is to help the individual learn who they are, what they want to do in life once they graduate, and to teach themselves or rather help them gain more knowledge and wisdom while attending classes, asking professors for assistance when needed, and participating in on-campus activities or organizations. This experience can be gained at any college; it just depends on the mindset of the individual attending.*

—KELSEY SANTIAGO, UNIVERSITY OF FLORIDA
(GRADUATE STUDENT IN FORENSICS)

Keep in mind that there are more than 3,000 four-year universities in the United States, which means that there are more than 300 schools that rank in the top 10%. The Ivies are a very small portion of the excellent universities out there. It's important, as a student, to keep an open mind about your options and the unexpected opportunities that you discover as you research and refine your own definition of what a dream school means for you.

# The Stats

According to worldatlas.com, there are close to 5,000 colleges and universities in the U.S. That's a lot of school options! This book will help you narrow down the choices.

Those 5,000 schools enroll more than 21 million students. If you are reading this, you will, no doubt, be one of those students soon. Know this: There is a school out there for you!

About 3,000 schools are four-year institutions and 1,700 are two-year. Most of the advice in this book comes from students pursuing a four-year degree. (The advice is just as relevant, however, if you are looking to begin your post-secondary education with a two-year program.)

Roughly 700 of the four-year schools in the U.S. are public; the 2,300 others are private, and their sizes range from very small (fewer than 500 students) to very large (more than 50,000 students). If you're not sure what type of school is right for you yet, keep reading!

You will see schools ranked according to all different criteria—admissions statistics, athletics, social scene, campus beauty, graduation rates, job placement, and more. The rankings from College Board, *U.S. News & World Report, Princeton Review,* and *Niche.com,* for example, can give you an idea of how you might begin to evaluate your own college options, but in the end, they don't mean as much as how you feel about a certain school and what it has to offer you. Your Top 10 list should look different from everyone else's because you create it for and about you.

What do all of the numbers mean? That if you are a hard working student and you want to go to college, there is most certainly one out there for you. It also means that all of those schools are competing for students. They want to fill their lecture halls with their ideal mix of dream students just as badly as you want a spot in one of their dorms. Yes, the college application process can feel like a cutthroat, competitive, and stressful endeavor, but don't lose sight of the fact that there are multiple schools out there that would love to have you on their roster next fall. Following the advice in this book can help you stand out as more than just a number and show your dream school all that you have to offer.

# Good Luck on Your Journey

The path from high school to college is a slow and steady kind of progression. You can't rush the acquisition of knowledge; the practice required to excel in a sport, musical instrument, or special interest; or the hours logged in community service. At times, the days, weeks, and months of school can seem endless. You may think you have plenty of time to improve your grades, study for those exams, earn a leadership role on a team, or win an award in a club. But before you know it, you'll be heading up to the podium to collect your high school diploma on your way to your dream school. How you get from here to there is up to you. Luck may be on your side, or not, but your level of hard work and determination is entirely within your control.

The process can also be stressful. Just remember to ask for help along the way when you need it. That's what this book is all about—assisting YOU.

*I'd highly recommend people consider reaching out for help when they really need it. Asking for help is not a weakness, but rather a strength. There are people out there who want to help and who will help you if you just ask for it. Although the search is hard and the application process stressful, no one ever said one has to accomplish it alone.*

—ABBIGAL MAENG, AUSTIN COLLEGE

# The Wisdom of Your Peers

At the same time that I was writing this book, I was evaluating "How I Got Into My Dream College" scholarship submissions. I remember thinking to myself, "These students could almost write this book themselves!" I always knew I would include real students' college application essays in the book, but thought that the advice and guidance would come mostly from experts in the industry. What emerged was the realization that the advice from students often mirrored or deepened the insight from the professionals. In reality, students who have recently been through the college application process have a perspective that makes them authorities on the subject. The following student—one of our scholarship winners—aptly describes her journey as a scramble through a complex and intricate jungle gym, rather than a straight climb up a ladder. Her "pearls of wisdom" give a taste of what is to come in the rest of the book. Real students, real stories.

PEARLS OF WISDOM

DOWN THE SLIDE AND ACROSS THE MONKEY BARS: CLIMBING THE JUNGLE GYM TO WELLESLEY COLLEGE

CASSANDRA ALLEN, WELLESLEY COLLEGE (CLASS OF 2018)

Sheryl Sandberg, in her incredible ability to sum up many of the life experiences of professionals across the globe, once noted that: "Careers are a jungle gym, not a ladder." While Sandberg was specifically speaking about the professional realm, I couldn't help but see the parallels between Sandberg's observations and my own college application process. In reflecting back upon my four years at Wellesley College and the incredible (and sometimes daunting) application process that preceded it, there was no clear-cut pathway from a small suburban Indiana high school to a celebrated women's college just outside of Boston. Instead, there were many adventures (and misadventures), a jungle gym if you will, that brought me to my home-away-from-home. In describing my own personal journey to the school of my dreams, I hope to capture and share my "pearls of wisdom" that I learned along the way and have the honor of sharing my story (with all of its successes and failures) with you.

The beginning of my college journey can be traced back to my sophomore year. As the oldest of three children raised in suburban Indiana, I was dying to explore outside of my small town and see what college adventures lay ahead. My parents spent fall breaks and winter vacations driving me around to different campuses within the state so we could do campus tours. While I was open to visiting Indiana schools, I was far more passionate about being out-of-state; however, before being allowed to explore outside of Indiana, my family wanted me to understand what local schools were available first. For my interest in fashion, I was already certain that no university in Indiana would have the program and connections that I needed to be successful; however, this assumption didn't hold true. While I didn't find the perfect fashion program within the state, I did learn other notable qualities to look for when visiting out-of-state schools. Particularly, I was enchanted by the beauty of DePauw's art museum and having an inspiring creative space such as that became an important characteristic for me. Additionally, I wanted an institution with a nice athletic facility (since I'm an avid runner) and a library that I could get lost in (being in atmosphere with good aesthetics helps me study better, or so I learned from my visits). Thus, from this experience comes my first pearl of wisdom: ***Start local, explore the different institutions around you. Even if you're absolutely certain that they aren't the right fit, you may just learn something unexpected about yourself and what is important to you in your college search.***

From an academic perspective, my focus in high school was to explore as many subjects as I could. I went through many different changes in terms of what I wanted to do professionally: everything from orthodontist, to fashion designer, to surgeon. This was hugely helpful in terms of forcing me to explore different subjects. And while I'm sure it was confusing to those around me who got a different answer as to what I wanted to do each time they asked, I'm incredibly grateful that it played out this way (because college is a jungle gym not a ladder!). I explored coursework in French, Math, English, History, Business, Science, and Art just to keep it all balanced, and whenever there was an Honors or AP option available, I attempted to pursue it. Ironically, after my first semester of college, I decided I no longer wanted to pursue fashion and instead switched to law and politics (which I am still studying to this day as I embark upon my master's degree this fall)! The pearl of wisdom from these experiences: ***Don't limit your-self. There are so many incredible possibilities out there, and you don't have to have everything figured out in high school. Explore, explore, and then explore some more—you never know what's going to prove valuable someday.***

The next journey that played a huge role in my college application adventure was my extracurricular experiences. I spent my first two years exploring everything that the school had to offer and my last two years devoting myself to my favorites of all of those clubs and sports. My first year, I joined the dance team and ran track and cross country before realizing that three sports was just too much for me. Following my first year, I kept just cross-country and track, and ultimately became a captain my senior year. My experiences as a runner helped me to hone my leadership capabilities and learn to time manage as I balanced sports and academics on a daily basis. But most of all, it gave me a family of sisters I could talk to and get advice from throughout every step of my high school career. In track I raced the 800m event, and our coach used to give us a particular strategy for racing that distance: "The first 200m you just have to find your place, the second 200m you have to maintain that new-found place, the third 200m you work harder than you've ever worked before, and the fourth 200m has a way of taking care of itself." Strikingly, the same strategy is true for high school and the application process: ***The first year you simply focus on figuring out where you fit in, the second year you try and maintain your place and deepen your friendships and academics, the third year you work harder than you've ever worked before applying to colleges while still being a student, and the fourth year (and your college future) has a way of taking care of itself.***

Outside of athletics, I explored an array of clubs and activities from Student Council, to DECA Business Club, to Key Club, to National Honor Society and French National Honor Society to, of course, the National Society of High School Scholars. Joining the clubs early helped me to determine exactly which clubs that I wanted to help lead someday: DECA and Student Council. My experiences on the

Executive Board of Student Council and DECA helped me to learn incredibly valuable lessons in leadership that shaped my extracurricular leadership in college. As an illustration, I once took on the role of Public Relations Coordinator and tried to do all of the announcements, posters, and publicity for all StuCo events alongside my five-person committee—that was way too much for one already overburdened junior. I learned, rather painfully, that there are limits to my capabilities even when I wish there were not and that I should respect them. From these anecdotes, comes my fourth pearl of wisdom: **You don't have to do everything; it's okay to pick one or two clubs and be passionate about them**.

Perhaps the most influential part of my college application journey was the summer that I spent living in France in between my junior and senior year of high school. Through the Indiana University Honors Program in Foreign Language, I was able to spend a summer living in Brest, France, with a host family and attending school. It was, by far, the scariest thing that I have ever done. Embarking upon the journey, the longest amount of time that I had ever spent outside of the country was a week over spring break and my French was good, but far from fluent. I had decided to try the program upon a recommendation from a cross-country teammate, and soon found myself thousands of miles from home living with a family that I could barely understand. That summer became my most challenging yet best summer ever. I grew as a student and as an individual, eventually becoming acquainted with my new home and new language/culture. It challenged my identity as an American, forcing me to re-examine my world through both French and American lenses. This experience was so impactful that it became the subject of my Common App personal essay and fostered a love for the French language, which I continued to pursue throughout college. Like many of the experiences that led me to Wellesley College, this summer was rather happenstance. I had wanted to participate in the program to better learn French; however, I had no idea what impact it would have on my college application experience. As I skimmed through the different Common App essay prompts, the identity prompt kept jumping out as the perfect opportunity to discuss an experience that meant so much to me and truly shaped who I am as a student.

In preparing the list of colleges to which I was interested in applying, I selected nine schools, mostly located on the East Coast: Columbia, Yale, Princeton, Cornell, Barnard, Wellesley, Fordham, DePauw, and Indiana University. My sample was very heavily Ivy League, with Columbia ranked as my first choice (and the school to which I later chose to apply Early Decision). Given my interest in fashion at the time, I wanted to be near a large city and attend the "best" (translate: most prestigious, if I'm speaking honestly) school that I was accepted into. Columbia seemed like the perfect fit, as did Wellesley and Barnard given their locations. My intended major didn't play as large a role in determining exactly where I applied because, as I understood it, you could study many things and go into fashion. My best pearl of wisdom from this selection process: **As cliché as it is, aspire high. Take risks and wherever you end up will be phenomenal.**

Managing applications for nine schools was tricky. I had a full excel spreadsheet of requirements that I used to keep track of due dates, recommendation letters, test score requests, and everything that would be needed to finish each application. It was both expensive and timely, but I managed to Early Decision one school and apply Early Action to two others (Wellesley and Fordham). In reflecting back, I don't think it was necessary to apply to as many schools as I did, especially considering that I wasn't all that excited about some of the schools on my list. As a pearl of wisdom, **I would wholeheartedly encourage applicants to apply only to schools that they're truly interested in attending and not just apply to schools, like I did, to have all of their bases covered.**

Just after I finished my applications, I traveled out to New York and Boston to do a final round of college visits. While I had visited Columbia before, I hadn't yet stepped foot onto Barnard, Wellesley, or Yale. Midway through my tour of Wellesley College, I can remember feeling overwhelmed by the beauty and warmth of the campus and jokingly remarking to my mother that I hoped Columbia didn't accept my application because I had decided that I wanted to go to Wellesley instead. Fortunate or otherwise, my joking wish came true: while I was crushed at the time, my rejection from Columbia opened the door for me to reconsider Wellesley.

My entire spring semester of my senior year was spent waffling between attending Wellesley College or Barnard College. Both schools were women's colleges, and both were located in large cities (Boston and New York, respectively). Both held unique characteristics that I had been searching for: art museums, beautiful libraries, nice athletic complexes, and natural beauty. While I was nearly certain that I wanted to be in New York at Barnard, Wellesley offered both degrees that I wanted: International Affairs and French while Barnard only offered one (French). While all of my friends had long ago made up their minds about where they wanted to attend, I sat there waffling and indecisive until the night before the May 1st commitment deadline. I sought out advice from my high school guidance counselors, but having not been heavily involved in my application process, they didn't offer much notable aid. After a short conversation with my parents (who told me to go with my gut feeling and that they would support whatever decision I made), I chose Wellesley, the campus that I had fallen in love with just a few months earlier.

Having made my decision, I've never looked back. Wellesley has been a place of tremendous exploration, growth, and happiness for me. She's given me opportunities that I wouldn't have otherwise had and challenged my perspectives in so many ways. The pearl of wisdom from this very long-winded anecdote is that: **The place where you're meant to be and the place that you think you want to be may not be the same.** For me, there was no direct path from high school to applying Early Decision to being accepted at that school. Instead there were many "plot-twists" that forced me to reconsider and re-examine the opportunities that confronted me. It took a full-out rejection letter before my eyes were fully opened to the perfect fit that Wellesley College was for me. College applications aren't always a clear-cut path, a ladder up and up if you will. They're a hot mess of a jungle gym that will eventually lead you to just precisely where you're meant to be.

Reflecting back on my application experience and college experiences in general, I have one overarching pearl of wisdom that has guided me through even the toughest of days (looking at you, summer in France). Will Smith, in his ability to pithily capture the nuances of life, once remarked that: **"Everything you've ever wanted is on the other** *side of fear."* Mr. Smith has succinctly summed up all that I could have hoped to pass along in this essay. There are so many incredible opportunities out there; we just have to be bold enough to go out and find them. Your college application process may not go as you have it planned out, and there's nothing wrong with that. It takes such incredible valiance to even begin, to put yourself out there. It takes even more courage to move to a new environment, to make new friends, to try new hobbies and clubs and sports. I spent so many sleepless nights worrying about what Wellesley would be like: Would I have any friends? What if the academics are really hard? What if I'm homesick? What if I don't like it? All of these feelings are real, and the fear itself was real, but the true joy was overcoming those obstacles and finding a school where I was challenged academically, yet still felt like I belonged. Everything I had ever wanted was there, on the other side of that fear. And so, future applicant, go out and conquer. Take risks, yet don't fret, because you will end up where you're supposed to be, and there will be so much more there than you ever could have imagined. Your application process may not be a clear ladder from high school to college, but it will guide you through your fear to exactly where you are meant to be.

# How to Make the Most of Your High School Years

Since you are reading this book, it means that you are already gazing out the windows of your high school, dreaming of the possibilities of college. You are looking to the future and all that it could bring. Congratulations, because that is the first positive step to get you to where you want to be. Though colleges rarely look at any data (grades, standardized test scores, activities) before ninth grade, they do care about your growth and accomplishments across all four years of high school. Making the most of that time can give you an edge so give yourself bonus points if you are a freshman just entering that phase. The following advice can help you maximize your efforts. If you are late to the college-prep party, don't fret. Just pick up the tips that you can use to give you a boost toward your goal.

# Create a Four-Year Plan

Though most students are actively working on the college search and application by the time they reach their junior year, it is important to at least start thinking about college (not the applications, just what your goal is) as early as freshman year. This will help to keep you motivated and prevent you from realizing too late that grades are a crucial part of a robust application.

*Freshman year of high school is when I really started thinking about college. Everyone says those four years of high school go by so quickly and you don't believe them as a freshman but then in a blink of an eye, you're nearing graduation and realize they were right. It is never too early to think about college!*

—NATALIE CHANDLER, BAYLOR UNIVERSITY
(FIRST-GENERATION STUDENT)

Kevin Qualls, a graduate student at Brown University, pursuing a Master's in Data Science, and a graduate of University of Southern California with a B.S. in Mechanical Engineering, offers advice about the benefits of planning ahead.

KEVIN QUALLS,
UNIVERSITY OF SOUTHERN CALIFORNIA
(CLASS OF 2018)
BROWN UNIVERSITY (GRADUATE STUDENT)

I first started preparing for college when I was a freshman in high school. Not to say I was studying for the SAT my freshman year, but I made an effort to meet with my counselors as often as possible, to make sure I was taking the right classes, as well as participating in the right clubs. Having the dream to go to college my freshman year was so critical, because it set the standard for the rest of my high school years. I unfortunately had many friends who began dreaming of attending college their senior years of high school, but by then, it was too late; their only options were two-year community colleges. If college is the goal, then one should start working for it as soon as high school starts.

Additionally, I recommend for a high school student to have an idea of what to pursue as a major in college by their sophomore year. For example, when I was a sophomore in high school, I decided my major in college would be engineering. To show college admissions officers my commitment to engineering, I took engineering courses at a vocational school my sophomore and junior year—in addition to attending my regular high school. I also interned for the UCLA Chemical Engineering Department the summer before my senior year, through a minority STEM program. As a result, my college application and personal statement had more credibility, and proved to admissions officers I wouldn't drop out of this intense major. It's best to be committed to a major during high school, but it's totally fine if a student switches majors in college for whatever reason—no shame at all.

A four-year plan doesn't have to be incredibly detailed, it can just be a blueprint for the courses you will take, the sports and activities you are interested in pursuing, and any other goals for making the most of your high-school years. It will also help you accomplish any course requirements or expectations that your dream schools have for applicants. Not all schools publish their minimum requirements, but many do. Princeton, for example, does not have strict high school course requirements for applicants, but its website states that most applicants' transcripts include the following courses:

- Four years of English (including continued practice in writing)
- Four years of mathematics (including calculus for students interested in engineering)
- Four years of one foreign language
- At least two years of laboratory science (including physics and chemistry for students interested in engineering)
- At least two years of history

- In addition, most candidates have had some study in the visual or performing arts.

Though minimum course requirements are general guidelines, the consensus among colleges is that it is best to take the most challenging courses that your school offers and that you can manage.

Kimberly Tyson, admissions liaison for Alberta University adds, "Getting into your first-choice college is very doable; the key is to create an action plan that will help bring your dreams to fruition. The most important aspect of your plan should be to access how you measure up with the admissions requirements of your dream college. Work with your teachers and guidance counselors to seek out resources if need be to boost your academic profile, finding extra-curricular activities, assistance with writing essays, practicing for college interviews, and finding references to attest to your academic achievements and accomplishments."

If you know what field/major you want to enter, be sure to prioritize taking higher-level (Honors, AP) classes in that area to best prepare yourself.

Your plan can change and evolve over the years. Here is a simple template that you can use or modify to get your own plan started.

| Four-Year Plan | Grade 9 | Grade 10 | Grade 11 | Grade 12 |
|---|---|---|---|---|
| English | | | | |
| Math | | | | |
| Sciences | | | | |
| History | | | | |
| Foreign Language | | | | |
| Arts | | | | |
| Sports | | | | |
| Activities/Clubs | | | | |
| Jobs | | | | |
| Volunteering | | | | |

According to College Counselor Michael Koenig at Proctor Academy in Andover, New Hampshire, "The four-year 'working' plan is an essential part of the college admission process. Designing a potential pathway through high school allows you to anticipate changes in your adolescent landscape with less stress as interests and passions ebb and flow. The secret ingredient is the balancing act between rigor and success. This means you need to dovetail your high school graduation requirements with the admission requirements at your colleges of current interest. Additionally, if you have a passion or talent in the arts or athletics, you should be aware of artistic portfolio requirements as well as the requirements of the NCAA Eligibility Center. Yes, you need to feel challenged, but do not underestimate the power of finding academic success as this can be a strong stabilizing factor in your well-being. Creating an overzealous four-year academic plan is a recipe for disaster! Remember, this is not a rigid plan chiseled in stone. It is a malleable document that requires vision and updating. High school is short, and you should feel in control of your destiny. And, by the way, you should be having a little fun along the way!"

How you make the most of your time and the available opportunities is entirely up to you. Here is one high-achieving student's story and advice:

SHANAYA SIDHU

UNIVERSITY OF CALIFORNIA, LOS ANGELES (UCLA)

I worked hard in high school to expose myself to different experiences that would prepare me for the rigors of college. I pushed myself as hard as I could in taking AP, honors, and even some college courses. I took a total of 14 AP exams, 4 honors courses, and 2 college courses throughout high school. Since I was interested in a medical career, I made sure to take rigorous science courses, such as AP Biology, AP Chemistry, AP Psychology, and Honors Anatomy/Physiology. While it is important to take as many AP courses as you can in order to challenge yourself, it is also very important to take AP courses in subject matter you are truly interested in, especially that which you are interested in pursuing in college. You will excel particularly in subject matter you are passionate about and driven by. The two college courses I took were Dance Appreciation, which I took in order to get one of my general education courses out of the way for free, and Medical Terminology, which I took in order to showcase my interest in medicine. I also took multiple SAT subject exams (Biology, Chemistry, United States History, World History, Math 2) to showcase my well-rounded background and interest in sciences to colleges. Outside the classroom, I also immersed myself in rewarding experiences that would provide me leadership and service opportunities. For example, I was a number one doubles varsity tennis player and a volunteer at multiple of my coach's tennis camps for younger children. I volunteered often, took part in a youth leadership program, and was a peer tutor. I was President of the Interact Club, Vice President of American Red Cross Club, and also a member of various clubs, such as California Scholarship Federation, National Honor Society, and Health Occupations Students of America.

Outside of school, I was a representative for my high school on the Simi Valley Youth Council, a member of a Relay for Life team with my friends, and a shadow at Los Robles Hospital during one of my high school summer breaks. I also worked at Kumon and had a passion for writing and poetry. It may seem like a lot but looking back on high school, all of it passed by so quickly. I was busy, but I also learned valuable time management skills and went through so many enriching experiences. All of these experiences eventually paid off as I got into a lot of great schools and received a lot of great scholarships, such as the Regents' Scholarship at UCLA. **It is better to keep yourself busy during high school with activities that interest you and help you make an impact on your community; you should always involve yourself in activities that benefit and interest you, rather than activities you think will interest colleges on your college resume. This is because colleges can see when you are just trying too hard to impress them, so you should showcase your passions through activities that you were dedicated to and made a difference in.** This will also help you when you have to write college essays about some of these experiences. For example, I led a project through Interact Club to plant a peace pole on our high school campus. It was an amazing experience for an issue I am passionate about, and this passion and commitment is what truly shined in my applications, not the project itself.

**Expect to Grow and Change.** As you work your way through your years of school you will experience phenomenal physical, intellectual, and emotional growth. Each year will build on the next; each accomplishment will prepare you for a greater goal. You won't suddenly pop out of high school fully formed with a long list of honors and AP credits. It's an evolution and everyone develops in a wholly individual way and at his or her own pace. This next student tells the story of her evolution from a shy little girl to a strong young woman ready to spread her wings at Dartmouth.

METAMORPHOSIS

SOLEIL GAYLORD,
DARTMOUTH COLLEGE (EARLY DECISION)

The first steps in my journey began in my rising freshman year. I was like a tight-fisted rose bud ready to unclench my petals one by one. I had big plans and big work ahead. My feet never touched the ground until I graduated. Stanford and Colorado College were the top schools on my dream college list. I had visited the Colorado College campus three times through middle school and into my high school years, and I loved the biology department, the block schedule, the extension campus in the San Luis Valley and the Colorado mountain background where I could run. I had an inclination for the natural sciences, especially environmental and biological studies. Stanford University was my "reach" dream school. Several of my family friends were Stanford graduates and I was impressed with these individuals as well as what the school represented and the immense opportunities in biology and scientific research. I was awed by the prestige and the opportunities of earning a degree from one of the top universities in the world with the world's greatest intellectuals as teachers. The evolution of my dream school(s) did change dramatically as the horizons and opportunities expanded in my senior year. The process, however, of getting into "that" dream school (whichever one it may be) involved my concentration in four major areas. I did my very best in each: Academics, Athletics, Community Service, and Extracurricular Activities.

Academics were the foundation of my four-pronged strategy to get into my dream school. My strategies were entirely self-created. My counselors had very little involvement in my *entire* college selection and application process, other than filling out the required counselor report and advising me to take AP courses. My parents and older sister in attendance at Smith College provided advice and helped me when I asked. Living in a remote rural town I did not attend college fairs. I started a spreadsheet in my rising freshman year using the state high school, my own high school's mandated requirements, and the AP/Honors courses offered at my high school as my guide. I used one page for each academic year and penciled in my four-year plan so that all my requirements were met. I focused on AP courses that I thought I would enjoy the most, including AP Environmental Science, AP Art, and AP U.S. History, and I substituted AP courses wherever I could for required regular classes like World History. I never took a regular required class if there was an AP alternative. I made sure to have at least three years of a language. I took honors classes that were offered in science courses I enjoyed. I thoughtfully plotted my APs so that I took one more AP class each year starting with one in my freshman and ending with four in my senior year. This resulted in a grand total of 10 APs upon graduation. This strategy showcased me as a student taking the most challenging courses with a heavy AP and honors load. I think this was smart for me because it balanced the number of AP courses against my intellectual capability, which improved and developed over the four years to the point that I could gracefully handle four APs in my senior year. Furthermore, using this stair-step tactic, I was able to score 5s and 4s on the final AP exams, which added strength to my application. In regards to the "regular" non-AP or non-honors classes, I was acutely aware of my GPA and kept constant vigil on the student portal to make sure I maintained a 4.0 in all my classes. If I felt I was slipping below my 4.0 unweighted GPA, I met teachers in the morning to get extra help. The academic aspect of my high school experience was the most important. I made sure to prioritize my grades above *everything* else in high school and to always achieve the A. I carefully considered the balance of taking the correct number of AP/Honors classes and earning As over taking too many difficult classes and getting mediocre semester grades. I worked hard and felt great pressure, but I created a balance in the coursework so that I was never *completely* over my head. I feel having a solid 4.0 unweighted GPA was an important first step to admission in my dream school.

Before beginning high school, I contemplated a four-year athletic plan and decided to focus on outdoor sports, specifically running sports that I could do all four seasons. These sports were fall cross country, winter snowshoe racing, spring track and mountain running in the summer. I also was interested in sports that were *both* an individual and a team sport. All four of the sports in which I competed were scored individually, but the individual points worked towards a team score. This team score was the frosting on the cake of my individual efforts and added much to the entire four years of competition from an emotional standpoint and also showing me to be a team player. In my rising freshman summer and every summer thereafter, I ran 600 miles through the mountains in preparation for an excellent freshman cross-country season. I did not wait for practice to begin in the fall and took self-initiative to be in excellent shape at the *beginning* of the season. Furthermore, those hundreds of miles of summer running earned me a seat on the prestigious U.S. Mountain Running team and I was able to compete internationally during one weekend of each cross-country season.

The international competitions were tremendously powerful from a cultural as well as competitive angle. They enriched my overall high school experience and added a bright star to that "list of achieve-ments" required on the Common Application and in resumes. When the snow started to fall, I strapped on my snowshoes and headlamp and ran up trails that led over avalanche chutes. I was in such good shape by December that I was able to earn two world titles in snow-shoeing during the winter season of my junior and senior years. I be-lieve this esoteric sport of snowshoeing added verve to my application showing me as a student that could think outside the box by pursuing a sport where I could actually take *advantage* of the bad weather and deep snow! This snowshoe fitness in turn, segued perfectly into my spring track season leading me to win state titles in distance events. These titles also built up my resume. Reflectively, I believe the athletic component of my quadruple-pronged strategy to getting into my dream school was a huge part of my success because it showed that I was a contributing member of four different teams, it meant that I had to be ultra-organized, and hugely motivated, it demonstrated to the admission committees that I was a hardworking and top caliber athlete *as well* as a top-notch academic. Lastly, being such a committed athlete just kept me physically fit which in turn aided my mental acuity.

During the summer of my rising freshman I began plotting out my individual service projects. I believed showing early foresight in these projects would be a *critical* aspect in strengthening my application helping me to get into my "dream school." That freshman summer, I designed and launched three community service projects that would span into my senior year, thus adding an element of integrity, duration, and commitment. A further benefit of starting community service work early is that it provided me rich literary fodder for the many essays that I would be writing for my college applications and scholarships. I deeply contemplated and planned out these projects and always had college essay ideas in my mind while working on them. I selected the projects taking specific criteria into consideration. These criteria included: creating a project that would cultivate my passion for botany/natural history/horticulture, creating service projects that had longevity, creating projects that would positively influence many community members, designing projects with a large "conservation quotient" that had significant local environmental educational impacts.

Lastly, I wanted each to be unique, yet tied into one common theme (environmental conservation) and I wanted them to be interesting to me and to the community. I created an agronomic, "healthy lifestyle" based peer-education program in the community greenhouse, I designed, created and maintain a native plant re-vegetation plot, and I created, produced and hosted my own local environmental radio show. I envisioned that if I did a good job at these service projects that I could be able to proudly hand them off to future rising freshmen giving them a chance to continue with a proven established service project. I was successful on all counts and my projects are solidly in place and integrated into my small town community. I'm carrying these projects through this summer and I have recruited a group of high school freshmen to carry the torches that I lit. It is also important to note, that I had a lot of fun while doing these projects and this fun was incorporated in my college essays making them easier to write and interesting, all-the-while showing off my passion in community service.

I was greatly involved in extracurricular activities including school clubs, organizations and self-generated studies. I began my involvement in my freshman year in these activities and emphatically believe that showing a four-year commitment was extremely important to improving my application and chances for acceptance to my dream school. I attended the first meetings of the Telluride High School Student Council at the beginning of my freshman year and was elected as an officer then and each year thereafter, until I was elected Student Body President for my senior year. Having three years of foundational experience also was a testament to my student government knowledge base and credibility of being the Student Body President.

Another tremendous benefit of being on the student council team was the strong relationships that I built with the teachers and the principal. These relationships enabled them to write me excellent letters of recommendation, and I was fortunate to have the principal write me a powerful and thorough letter of recommendation! I was a member of clubs that dovetailed with my environmental passion like the HOPE (Help Our Planet Earth) Club, and a language club that bolstered my ability to speak a second language. Another gutsy component of my application's extracurricular element was the mentorship programs that I created. I feel confident that this was a superb garnish that showcased my spontaneity, my relentless pursuit of knowledge and my creativity in seeking intellectual mentorship outside of the school faculty, engaging professionals within our community. This is the kind of stuff that top-notch universities probably like to see.

I designed my own political science mentorship with a local Stanford PhD scientist. We met at coffee shops and talked prohibition and Watergate. I received A mentorship credits, and had a blast while learning a fascinating part of history. I designed my own agrarian based mentorships and worked as a peer-educator in my school's greenhouse, getting community service hours, learning new gardening techniques and earning humanities credits all at once. All of these projects were close to my heart and fulfilling to me. Of final mention, I believe that creating my own *local, summer* work studies and scientific research projects and volunteering in *local, summer* community service projects helped to make my application stand out and demonstrated my cleverness and practicality. I never paid for expensive overseas "volunteer" experiences; instead I opted to demonstrate my practicality and ingenuity saving the money that would be spent on airfare and "course fees" and choosing to leave a lighter environmental footprint. This was done by creating local fundraisers, like my community art sale that I installed with all profits going to a pollinator conservation group. I also adopted a stretch of local highway and cleaned it for six years. My work was visible as locals saw me collecting trash, plus the Department of Transportation installed a sign imprinted with my name between my cleaned mile markers. I became one of my town's own eco-warriors. I believe all of these efforts added credibility to my application helping it on its way to the "accepted" pile.

My four-part strategy was neatly in place when I began my senior year. I had straight A's, had scored well on my SAT and my AP exams. I was Student Body President, a world champion snowshoe racer, an all-state runner, a five-time state champion runner, an Ambassador for the American Trail Runners' Association, and I was a Sportswoman of Colorado. I had articles about my community service work published in magazines. I had peer educated the bulk of the community. Then I began winning awards including the High School Heisman and the Congressional Award. The Claremonts and Ivies started courting me. I had no idea when I began my senior year and was thrilled! I made visits to Dartmouth, Pomona, Stanford, and Pitzer. I began to re-evaluate my dream school list and Dartmouth became my number one dream school. I made this decision after a three day visit to the campus. I sat in on the small classes and loved the seven to one ratio of students to faculty. I loved the engaging and friendly students that I met. I loved the Ivy traditions and the challenging Ivy curriculum. I loved the Ivy League ambience with the intimate feel of a small liberal arts school (an enrollment of just over 4000 students). I also appreciated Dartmouth's undergraduate focus with professors teaching classes and not graduate teachers' assistants. I also loved the surrounding mountains, the small town of Hanover, the Dartmouth Garden, the Dartmouth Sophomore Summer program, the cross country and track team, the semester abroad programs, the Environmental Studies with the possibility of a focus in glacier studies. I contemplated the enticing Writing and Rhetoric major. Everything seemed a perfect fit for me coming from a small, rural, Colorado mountain town. As further encouragement, once the word was out that I was considering Dartmouth as my top choice, Dartmouth alumni began to enthusiastically approach me, even knocking on my door to talk Dartmouth. Recently-graduated Dartmouth students that lived in my town arrived with desserts telling me they were at my service to answer any Dartmouth-related questions.

They proceeded to elaborate on their wonderful Dartmouth undergraduate experiences. My decision was becoming more and more solid.

I made a grid of all the schools on my wish list and with clear-headed decisiveness decided to apply Early Decision to Dartmouth. The pros column for Dartmouth had checkmarks all the way down. I put Stanford and Colorado College on my regular decision list and let them sit in the Common Application bin as future possibilities if I was rejected from Dartmouth. I wanted to apply early because I was serious about Dartmouth being my first choice and if I were accepted in December I would be done with the process of application. I had learned so much about myself, about the colleges I visited, about the process of decision-making and the clarity of that final moment. I was ready to commit to Dartmouth College. I paid the 80-dollar application fee, signed the binding decision agreement, and pressed the "Submit" button for Dartmouth Early Decision. It was November 1. I received a likely letter, which is a notification sent out to a small number of students before the formal decision date, shortly thereafter, and I was elated to be accepted to Dartmouth on December 15, 2017. I believe my application was bombproof on all levels. Echoed throughout this essay, the under-riding piece of advice that I offer to rising freshman as they begin their evolutionary journey through high school: Plan ahead and plan seriously and plan to work very hard, *before* beginning high school, it is a *four-year process.*

There were two short essay questions specific to Dartmouth that took me a few days to perfect while working on my Common Application. I believed that the essay component of my application had the potential of setting my application apart. In fact, I knew this throughout high school and so I created a folder with "essay ideas" that came to me when interesting events/thoughts happened. I drafted my Common App. essay during my rising senior summer because I anticipated senior autumn semester to be intense and I wanted to set aside a week to hone my 650 word essay. In August, I pasted the question at the top of my "Common Application Essay" Google doc and wrote three different essays answering it. The question read, "Some students have a background, identity, interest, or talent that is so meaningful they believe their application would be incomplete without it. If this sounds like you, then please share your story." I constructed a unique answer each time and one that showcased my endeavors while telling a story, always staying within the 650-word limit. I felt my essay represented me well and it read fluidly. It shares the same title of this essay because they both speak to the change and growth that happened to me on my path to adulthood:

## Metamorphosis

It took me 12 years to say "Good morning!" to Ms. Overly. Why? While my classmates had many goals—learning the meanings of new words or discovering the basics of math—my first grade goal never changed because I never achieved it. I was tasked with greeting my teacher daily: "Good morning, Ms. Overly." During preschool, kindergarten, and first grade, I had only spoken three words consecutively: tiger swallowtail butterfly. I accidentally blurted out the descriptor when a black-striped lepidopteron fluttered overhead; it was methodical for me to classify the insects I adored. This proclamation was shocking; I could speak. Like the "mute" Chief in "One Flew Over the Cuckoo's Nest" unwittingly murmuring, "Ah, Juicy Fruit" when McMurphy gifts him a stick of gum, my jig was up.

I could speak, yet I was too fearful to pupate and expose my still tightly-folded wings to adults. What the counselors didn't understand was that I "communicated" perfectly well with the natural world, and it didn't require words. The social worker called my disorder selective mutism, and placed me in a classification shared with two percent of other elementary-aged students. This was my nemesis and yet my baseline for improvement and change.

Gently my wings unfurled. The value of conversation, particularly with teachers, became increasingly apparent. Watching Food Inc. was required in our sixth grade agriculture unit; the film's message enraged me. I verbally engaged; I literally "found my voice" and spoke ardently in defense of subjects I loved. These uncharacteristic, but passionate discourses became increasingly frequent. In eighth grade,

I volunteered to be a "closer" for the debate team. Taking the stage, my hands quivering, I delivered a succinct speech arguing against the National Security Administration. The crowd applauded, parents complimented me, and our team won the issue. I felt emboldened.

I have overcome selective mutism entirely. I take pride in being a leader, acting upon issues in my community, defending what I love, and partaking in valuable discussion. I have taken wing and lead agronomy classes in our school's greenhouse; a program I founded and run called "Brownies to Broccoli." I teach nearly 350 students each year about the importance of a healthy lifestyle and the benefits of a plant-based diet. I present to the Telluride Ecology Commission regularly and provide updates regarding the progression of a native rare species plot I designed and maintain. I fly on as Senior Class President, cross country/track Captain, a four-time State Champion, a World Champion snowshoer, an athlete on the U.S. Mountain Running Team, and an American Trail Ambassador, committed to the fostering of trail running and outdoor enjoyment. I delighted in leading my team to two consecutive state titles; I mentor young athletes and promote the serious value of team camaraderie and incessant advancement toward a goal. With a graduate biology team, I research Gunnison's Prairie Dogs (an endangered yet extremely undervalued species), plotting their evolution and preservation.

I am a local radio show producer and share wildlife stories with the entire community, clarifying with guest biologists the common misconceptions held against certain species. I am poised as I deliver daily school announcements over the loudspeaker and lead assemblies. A local restaurant owner and I collaborate in selling donated art for the Xerces Society; I was recently published for my outstanding work in the preservation of invertebrate species. Perhaps a metaphor for my proliferation, a monarch butterfly laid eggs this fall on the plot. Declining Monarchs feed exclusively on the milkweed plant, which is being rapidly destroyed by monoculture farming. I propagated some milkweed myself, in an effort to provide a small parcel of precious habitat. Perhaps monarchs will hatch there and fly off, much like I have, on their long migration to Mexico. I can check off a hard-won goal, because I heartily greet Ms. Overly when she visits the greenhouse with her first graders.

**Honor Your Own Journey.** Not everyone is a straight A student, athletic superstar, and champion of their own community service legacy. You can certainly aspire for greatness in all of these areas. Be proud of the achievements you do make on your journey and always strive to try a little bit harder, learn a little bit more, push a little bit further toward your own individual goals. Other passions outside of the obvious ones are just as important and impressive. Admissions officers are looking for interesting students with unique interests, not just ones who achieve in academics, sports, and through volunteer work.

**Don't Judge.** Try not to look across the room at your classmates and judge them for the brilliance of their smiles. You never know what hardships they have endured, challenges they have overcome, or privileges they have been afforded. You. Never. Know.

**Stay true to yourself!** *I do not know about others, but it is so easy for me to get caught up in another person's business. Yet, it does not matter what others are doing, it matters what you are doing. Do you have a dream in your heart that was laid a long time ago, aching to hatch and be set free? Pursue it. Find a practical logical way to pursue it. Live your own life; you are after all on your way to a place that is supposed to help you grow into your own person.*

—EYRAM AKAKPO, UNIVERSITY OF AKRON

**Keep a Calendar—And Keep Track of It.** Whether you like your smart phone's calendar application or prefer to keep a written calendar or planner, find a way to track your classes, appointments, and deadlines, and check it each day. Cultivating the habit of keeping a calendar will be essential when it comes time to organize your college application materials and deadlines and will help you be successful for the rest of your life! Simply writing down your daily activities will help you remember them, and keeping your calendar can help you plan your study time so you never get behind in your classes.

## Master Your Mindset

Think big! Believing in yourself and having faith in what you can achieve will help you to be successful. Making this your mindset will help get you to where you want to be. Having a positive mindset helped me grow many successful organizations. It can also help you ace that test next week, meet your deadlines, gain acceptance into your dream school, and still have time for your friends.

A positive frame of mind is a powerful force. On the other hand, negative thought patterns can have toxic effects on your ability to think clearly, focus on your studies, and accomplish your goals. Get into the habit of giving yourself positive affirmations when you study like reminding yourself of how skilled you are on a particular topic. Avoid negative thinking and convincing yourself ahead of time that you're going to do poorly on a test. You're more likely to succeed if you think positively and enjoy yourself.

When you create positive associations with studying, you're more likely to continue doing it. Be sure to reward yourself when you have maintained your study schedule or reached a goal. Celebrate with a night out with friends, your favorite meal, going for a walk, or whatever else motivates you to stay clear and focused.

Also know that it's okay to take a break from studying if you aren't in the right mindset. There's only so much you can force yourself to do. When you are preoccupied with other things going on in your life then you're not likely to retain the necessary information. A simple change of scenery, a snack, an hour with friends or family can provide much-needed relief. When you do return to the task feeling refreshed and focused, you'll be better able to optimize the time.

No matter how positive you are, sometimes things won't go your way. You need to learn how to get back up and keep going when failure occurs. How you deal with difficulty will make a difference in your success.

# Academics: Making the Grade

One of the important aspects of your college application will be your Grade Point Average (GPA). You are going to want to score the highest grades possible in order to earn a spot at a competitive school. You will want those high achieving stats in the most challenging courses your school offers. Taking AP and honors classes is generally better than breezing through with straight A's in less challenging courses.

*AP classes show that you're prepared for college classes, and believe it or not, they actually prepare you for college work. Even if you don't make an "A" in these classes, taking these classes shows colleges that you like to challenge yourself and are willing to work hard.*

—ALI AL HAJAJ, NEBRASKA WESLEYAN, 3.918 GPA

The winners and finalists of our "Dream College" scholarship all reported impressive GPAs ranging from 3.0 to 4.4. Keep in mind that many colleges will recalculate GPA based only on core subjects alone, such as math, science, English, social studies, and foreign languages. So that A in gym class probably means you are fit and active, but it may not count for much on your transcript. College admissions typically value students with a difficult course load and grades that represent strong effort and upward trending scores. Many colleges will also award scholarships based on your GPA or SAT/ACT scores, so it pays to maximize those points (and dollars). Here are a few strategies to help:

## Take Advantage of Extra Credit

Though not all of your teachers will offer extra credit, make sure to take advantage of any opportunities your teachers do offer. Sometimes extra credit will come in the form of an extra paper, a book report, or an independent study project. You could even come up with an extra credit project idea of your own and pitch it to your teacher! Most teachers genuinely do want to see you succeed, so if they see you going out of your way to improve, they're likely to want to give you an opportunity to do just that. What they expect you to do will vary, but many teachers will offer you an opportunity for extra credit to help you boost your grade and improve your GPA.

## Participate in Class

It can be tempting to zone out in class, but don't underestimate the value your teacher places on class involvement. If you're right on the line between a C and a B, your teacher may be more likely to round up if you've been showing an active interest in class, asking questions, and being more involved. Raise your hand, volunteer to help set up an experiment, make eye contact with your teacher, and ask questions after class if you missed something.

## Find a Tutor

If you're really struggling in a particular class, it may be a good idea to find a tutor. It's never too late and having a tutor to help guide you can significantly raise your test scores, grade, and overall GPA. There is no shame in acknowledging the need for a tutor. In fact, the best students are often so strong because they rely on the help of a tutor.

## Seek Out Extra Help

Most teachers have free blocks or will offer to meet you after school for extra help. Be proactive about asking for that extra attention if you have questions or need clarification on concepts that you don't understand. This can also motivate you to get started on big projects or papers earlier in the semester instead of procrastinating until the night before. Not only can visiting your teacher for extra help improve your GPA, but it can also boost your reputation as a high-performing student in the same way that diligently participating in class can. Again, the best students often make a habit of asking for extra help. You want to be in that camp.

## Develop Good Study Habits

Improving your study habits can have a big impact on your test results. Start scheduling your study time much earlier than you think you need to and organize a study group with your classmates. Sometimes studying on your own can be harder than studying with a group. By forming a study group with other students in your class, you will have the power of more minds working together and might be more likely to commit to studying. Study groups are an opportunity to seek guidance from other students in the class who may understand the concepts that you're struggling with and can help you stay motivated.

## Make Up Any Missed Assignments

This is a no-brainer. Obviously, it's better to stay up-to-date with assignments, but if your teachers allow it, you can try to make up missed assignments throughout the semester that are hurting your overall grade. A zero calculated for a missing assignment can ruin your grade. Even if you will only receive partial credit for turning in a missing assignment late, it's worth it.

## Stay Focused

Keep your future goals in mind to motivate you. All your hard work will be worth it!

However your GPA and test scores are only one portion of your college application and many very competitive schools look at much more than just your academic achievements. Emily Pacheco, the Outreach and Admissions Specialist for the International Programs at UC Berkeley Extension says, "You have to stand out to get into UC Berkeley. We want interesting students, not just smart students. A student with a 4.0 GPA and 1550 SAT scores doesn't necessarily get admitted. UC Berkeley is not just looking for smart students, they are looking for interesting students!"

# Activities: Arts, Athletics, STEM, Community Service, Jobs, and Volunteer Work

One way to round out your resume is to participate in extracurricular activities. What you do outside of the classroom says a lot about who you are and what you care about. The activities you list on your resume and the stories you tell on your applications can help reveal those passions and pursuits. Meaningful use of your "free" time can encompass summer activities, hobbies and passions, or work that reflects areas of interest, responsibility, and dedication. Schools are looking to attract a diverse student body with special talents, unique skills, or experiences. They are also looking for evidence of your intellectual curiosity and eagerness to learn and grow. A high school student who goes beyond his or her academic endeavors to develop skills in cooking, journalism, artificial intelligence, or any other creative passions can gain an edge.

*You should get involved in as many clubs and/or sports as is possible without splitting yourself in two. School activities show colleges that you're a person who's attached to your school, isn't afraid to be a part of something bigger, knows how to work with other people, and is more than just a GPA.*

—ALI AL HAJAJ, NEBRASKA WESLEYAN

Most experts, however, caution students not to strive for a laundry list of extracurriculars to put on their resumes. You can stand out by displaying deep involvement in a few extracurricular activities, especially when they spark extreme passion and creativity.

*Select activities that you are actually interested in, and not just ones that you think an admissions officer would like. Being extensively involved in a handful of activities and holding leadership positions is better than being a "member" in as many as possible.*

—ARIF HARIANAWALA, UNIVERSITY OF TEXAS AT AUSTIN

A common recurring theme that colleges look for in students is depth, not breadth, of experience. Colleges like to see sharp and proficient students with focused passions, not necessarily well-rounded students who are marginally adept in many different things. In other words, substantive commitment to a few select activities is preferred over widespread participation in several activities that have minor significance.

The most important element to consider when choosing extracurriculars is YOU. Your personality, goals, dreams, and interests will lead you in the right direction when it comes to your perfect extracurricular activities. College and university admissions officers want to see that you have all the necessary qualities to succeed at their institution, but mostly they want to see who you are and what you can bring to their campus. Beyond the desire to get into college at any cost, the activities you choose to pursue in school should be a reflection of your greatest strengths and offer a looking glass into the kind of contribution you'll bring.

Colleges look for applicants who are involved, passionate, and proactive in the learning process inside and outside of the classroom. Our scholarship finalists were involved in a broad range of extracurricular activities—debate, dance, chess club, internships and jobs, music therapy, rocket science, community outreach, volunteering, and more—that helped them demonstrate the kinds of leadership skills and qualities admissions officers like to see on college applications.

## Show Commitment and Consistency

No matter what you decide to do, try to show an ongoing commitment and purpose to your endeavors. My father was the first in his upstate New York village in the Adirondacks to go to college. He went to the University of Michigan as a result of the GI Bill, became an engineer, and worked in the U.S. Army Corp of Engineers. My father instilled in me the idea that if I were going to make it in life I would have to work hard and prove myself. All through high school I worked many part-time jobs, including working at a local restaurant, at a gas station, and even mowing yards, so I didn't have time for any extracurriculars. I built up my mowing business by hiring my friends and eventually saved enough money to buy a little used VW and to pay for college. My dad didn't give me a penny, but he and my mom showed me unconditional love. My dad was very tough, and we weren't a wealthy family. He said I had to go out and do it myself. So I did. It was the best life lesson that has helped shape me into the person I am today. I was able to pay for my undergraduate university, back then a whopping $2,500 per year. The lessons and guidance my parents provided to me allowed me to establish the values and work ethic, which led me to achieve my master's degree, teach at the graduate level, and also have the honor to be the commencement speaker at my alma mater.

According to Russell Davis, the Director of Global Student Recruitment at Duke Kunshan University, showing that kind of progression and long-term commitment to your activities, jobs, and leadership roles is important. He says, "Applicants are understandably eager to demonstrate their wide range of interests and involvements to the Admissions Committee. Often times they will do this by listing a long list of activities and achievements in the extracurricular section of the application. However, what is more compelling to an application reader is to understand what are those activities, those interests and passions that are most important to the applicant. The Admissions Committee will be more impressed by seeing deeper involvement in a few activities as well as understanding why those activities are important to the applicant, including the inspiration for the interest and how the applicant may have grown as a result of their involvement. What did they learn about themselves? What skills did they grow through the experiences associated with the interest? Ultimately, a school wants to get to know the applicant not just as a candidate, but as a person. Helping the Admissions Committee understand what is important to the applicant and why is a great way to do that. Quality over Quantity!"

Here are just a few of the kinds of extra-curricular activities that you could consider.

**Debate.** High school debating teams are challenged to stay up-to-date with current news stories, government policies, and social issues, so students with debate experience often look attractive on college applications. Debate will help you learn to speak in front of people, formulate intelligent opinions, think critically, and connect the goings on of the world with the society you experience every day.

**Leadership Activities.** Extracurricular activities that require leadership, like student government, youth leadership conferences or intensives, and volunteer opportunities for local campaigns are attractive to colleges looking for the young leaders of tomorrow. Even if you have no plans to get involved with politics in the future, leadership skills are helpful for any major in college and will also serve you well throughout your adult life. Learning to be a leader will allow you to gain a better understanding of other people and their skills and will challenge you to inspire others through your own ideas.

**Academic Teams and Clubs.** Activities like Odyssey of the Mind, Quiz Bowl, Chess Club, and mathematics competitions show colleges and universities that you are competitive, passionate, and thoughtful. Academic teams and clubs also showcase your interest in academics outside of the classroom, which will be required of you more in college than in high school. By taking part in an academic team or club, you can demonstrate your ability to work hard, cooperate with a group of people, and perform difficult tasks under pressure. Your application will tell the story of a student not afraid of hard work.

**Creative Pursuits.** Artistic extracurricular activities like art clubs, theatre, music, and dance showcase your creativity and individuality. These are especially helpful for students who hope to pursue an artistic major, but extracurricular activities in the arts can show colleges and universities that you are well rounded and understand the value of the arts in society. Creative pursuits can be very rewarding and even stress-reducing throughout high school, which is another reason to consider an artistic activity if you have interests in the arts.

**Sports.** Being a talented athlete can definitely get students noticed by colleges, but you do not have to plan to play sports past high school for your sports experience to matter. Any athletic activity shows your determination, enthusiasm, and resilience—all qualities you need to succeed in any of life's endeavors. A team sports activity on a college application also communicates your ability to work well with others and be supportive in a group setting.

**Internships.** Though many students assume internships are reserved for college, if you find an opportunity to complete an internship in high school, it could be a great addition to your resume. By following through with an internship, you are showing college admissions officers that you can work effectively under pressure and cooperate in an adult professional scenario. Internships also demonstrate that you are proactive and interested in trying new and sometimes difficult experiences in pursuit of your future goals.

**Community Outreach and Volunteerism.** Putting volunteering experiences on your college application might seem cliché after every advisor has told you over and over again to start volunteering more, but lending a helping hand to others will never go out of style. Whether you have the opportunity to volunteer abroad or have an interest in volunteering locally, community outreach is a wonderful way to show your greatest qualities on your college application. Find a cause you are personally passionate about, and start volunteering to make a difference. As a volunteer you can improve the world, feel good about the way you are spending your time, and showcase positive qualities on your college application: a win-win-win situation.

**Part-Time Jobs.** Believe it or not, college admissions officers also understand that high school students often have busy schedules and sometimes have to juggle part-time jobs with full-time school. If you find yourself without much time to pursue extracurricular activities because of a part-time job, know that the skills you are learning and the qualities you are showcasing at your job matter on your college applications as well. Keep track of lessons you feel you have learned on the job and take leadership opportunities when you can. All your experiences shape the person you are and will later become riveting subjects for college application essays.

**Prepare a Resume.** If you don't think you will need a resume until you are ready to apply for a job, think again. Not only is a resume a great way to keep an organized account of all your activities and accomplishments, it will also help you when it comes time to apply for college and scholarships. When preparing your college applications, a detailed outline or resume will showcase any extracurricular activities or meaningful involvement you've had outside the classroom. Resumes can follow many different formats. Turn the page to view a sample resume from one of the "Dream School Scholarship" finalists.

Whatever you decide to do, do it well, and commit fully. College admissions officers like to see students who have passion and dedication. Do not feel the need to take part in every activity; choose one or two you love, dive in deep, and enjoy!

**Student Resume**
Sydney Price

**Student High School/College Achievements**

- Elected Parliamentarian of Georgia Future Business Leaders of America 2015-2016
- Member of Georgia BETA club
- Student Ambassador for National Society of High School Scholars
- Full-Time Move On When Ready/Dual Enrollment Student at Middle Georgia State University
- Nominated for the National Academy of Future Physicians and Medical Scientists Award of Excellence
- 2016 Graduate of Laurens Youth Leadership
- 3.6 GPA
- Member of Dublin High School Danceline 2014-2015
- Member of Dublin High School Irish Madness Dance Team 2016-2017
- Certified Gifted Student through the Dublin City School System
- Selected as At-Large Representative for the 2017-2018 Laurens County Youth Council
- Made the Dean's List for the 2016 Fall Semester at Middle Georgia State University
- Top 5% of the Dublin High School 2018 Graduating class
- Dublin High School Honor Graduate
- Awarded with the Class of 2018 Georgia Certificate of Merit.
- Leading volunteer prosecutor for Dublin - Laurens County Teen Court
- 2018 Dublin – Laurens County Youth of the Year
- Accepted to Spelman College class of 2022
- GA Secretary of State Student Ambassador
- Part time sales associate at Rainbow Store in Dublin Mall
- Summer 2018 intern for Dublin City
- First Place Winner of the Dublin Laurens County Oratorical Contest

**Additional Achievements**

- Two-time published author in poetry book for Texas Library of Poetry
- Member of Greater Macedonia's Youth Choir and Praise Team

**Volunteer Work/ Community Service (Total Hours: 206)**

- Dedicated 96 hours volunteering for Dublin, Georgia VA Medical Center
- Volunteer prosecutor for Dublin – Laurens County Teen Court 2016-present day (spent 72 hours volunteering from January 2016 – June 2017)
- Volunteered in "Female Veterans Tribute" at Middle Georgia State University 2017 (2 volunteer hours)
- Volunteered at "Suicide Prevention Youth Rally" at Oconee Fall Line Technical College 2017 (4 volunteer hours)
- Leader of the Promposal Fundraising Project Raffle for Dublin High School through FBLA 2015-2016 (4 hours)
- Participated in the St. Patrick's, Martin Luther King, and Christmas parades throughout 2015-2016 (18 volunteer hours total)
- Participated and Volunteered in a Cancer Walk/Program for cancer survivors created by my Dublin High School BETA club in 2016 (6 volunteer hours)
- Volunteered with Habitat for Humanity (2 hours)
- Volunteered at a local soup kitchen (2 hours)

## It's Not Rocket Science—Unless You Want It to Be

The main point of this section title is that your path to the college of your dreams will be defined by the goals you set for yourself. Some of you may thrive on competition and pressure. Others will prefer a lower stress or more supportive environment. While it is always good to challenge yourself, it doesn't have to be so difficult that you are miserable.

Felix Morales's story, which literally involves rocket science, shows how passion, lofty goals, and focused perseverance can lead to a successful outcome.

FELIX MORALES,
FLORIDA INSTITUTE OF TECHNOLOGY

When I was eight years old, I visited NASA Kennedy Space Center in Cape Canaveral, Florida. From that moment on I started to be obsessed with building, designing and creating things. In 9th grade, my love for science grew, and I decided that the career I wanted to pursue was aerospace engineering and helping mankind to travel to the stars. I got involved in STREAM (Science, Technology, Robotics, Engineering, Arts, and Mathematics), kept watching Space Shuttle Launches on YouTube, and started researching aeronautical engineering schools.

Once I decided where I really wanted to pursue my interests, I talked to my school counselor for college prep tools and to my parents about ways to enhance my resume with extracurricular activities, voluntary work, and research opportunities. I thought it would be a great idea to enter the school science fair to demonstrate my abilities since I wanted to create innovations that could solve a problem in any aspect of society. When I started my research, I fell in love with Magnetic Levitation (Maglev) technology. I wanted to create a "Maglev" system to improve the highway transportation systems by reducing emissions and using a high-speed highway as a means of daily transport. At first, my experiments and science fair entries did not succeed and I became discouraged. I continued to work on my research until I successfully levitated a model car about 7 cm from the ground. I was so amazed that I decided to participate in another science fair and demonstrate how my research worked. This time around, I succeeded, and I made it to the Intel International Science and Engineering Fair in Pittsburgh, Pennsylvania, along with approximately 2,000 students competing worldwide. During the special awards, I won the sustainable design transport award. In 11th grade, I competed again with a new Maglev research project. This consisted of an advanced Maglev runway suspension system to land military, commercial, and space aircraft to reduce the number of landing accidents and save the lives of hundreds of passengers. As I competed again, companies such as NASA, CERN, and the U.S. Navy were interested in my research. I was also awarded the Boeing Scholarship to study in the United States. Due to the positive outcome, I've started to obtain patents for my research to continue my project at a research university in the future. Once I was recognized by members of local Puerto Rico science institutions, I started being involved in a series of internships and research institutions. Between 2015-2017 I participated in a series of competitions involving designing, building, and launching reusable-hybrid rockets for my school. I also participated in an internship for Honeywell Aerospace in the Polytechnic University of Puerto Rico Rocket Laboratory. I also participated in summer camps such as Techno Inventors and won competitions involving Submergible Robotics. Also, I participated in extracurricular activities and talents such as Saxophonist of the School Band at Mita Congregation School. I passed the exams to be certified as a Microsoft Office Software Specialist. Moreover, I managed to be involved in voluntary work that helped me make a change in my community and also gave me access to scholarships and other financial help. I decided to start my own community foundation called: "Technology at your reach" to help students with the lowest incomes in Puerto Rico access better STREAM education through the robotic building, computational design, and video game programming. My program ended with more than 100 hours of service and expanded into other low-income communities across all Puerto Rico and some nearby islands like U.S. Virgin Islands and the Dominican Republic. I also participate in the creation of a Biomedical Smart Computer Gadget for kids with special needs and physical disabilities. The project was founded by my own high school and we managed to design, build, produce, and give the "Tech hand" to SER of Puerto Rico Disabilities Students Facility. Finally, these key extracurricular aspects helped me get closer towards my college admissions process and be finally admitted into a top-tier aerospace school.

# Time Management

For some reason the idea of being a stressed-out student has become romanticized in movies and on television shows, but do not be fooled. Being stressed out is not enjoyable and is not necessary. During an expert panel at an NSHSS Scholars' Day event in Washington, D.C., recruiters and diversity specialists at several major companies spoke about the qualities they look for in employees. Time management skills bubbled to the top of the list. It is also a recurring theme on college campuses across the country. Learning how to make the most of the time you have available will help you achieve your goals.

Robert A. Marchman, Executive Vice President, Financial Industry Regulatory Authority, recalls, "When I went to college, I was a first generation student and didn't have a lot of guidance. I took a time management course that has, to this day, helped me in my career. Specifically, you learn to take account of how you are going to spend your day. And you do so in a very proficient and effective way. And if you do that you find that you'll have more time for things that you want to do. That elective course was instrumental to my success. It provided me with the discipline; it can break you out of the habit of procrastination. You have to look for ways to decompress and reduce stress and time management can help."

Torrence Traynham, Global Diversity & Inclusion TA Lead, Marsh & McLennan Companies adds, "Rise early, wake up early, clear your mind, focus your day. You only have so much energy and so much time in a day so make sure you prioritize what's important. Make sure that when you start something you see it through to the end so when you complete something you can tie a bow on it and move on to the next thing."

Rather than procrastinate and cram before each test or major assignment, take the time to study course material over weeks and months. Our brains love being primed for information. Before each class, take the time to review past material and preview upcoming material in your textbook so your brain is ready and willing to take in the information you are about to learn. Take detailed but organized notes during class, and go over them once after class is rough to solidify the information.

Turn your notes into a study guide long before your test, and when you do need to study a little extra before the big day of an exam or even a presentation, you will have all the information organized and ready to absorb. This tip will help you avoid the unappealing task of running around trying to gather notes from friends or re-read the entire textbook one last time. Understandably, you might still feel slightly nervous for the test, thanks to your body's fight or flight response, but you will have already been studying and will feel much better than if you put the whole ordeal off until the very last week—or even day—before a test.

If you know you have a big paper or project due in a class at the end of the term, take the time to read the prompt ahead of time. As you get ideas while you are learning valuable information in the class, write them down. By the time you are ready to write the paper or complete the project, you will have a whole brainstorming list at the ready.

CHRISTIAN CHAMBERS,
HAMPTON UNIVERSITY

Managing my time was extremely challenging. I had to balance my academics, scholarships, sports, helping take care of things at home, and college applications. As a senior scholar and a senior athlete taking both Advanced Placement and Honors classes, I was extremely drained. My time management came into play when I started to get up early. I also had to start writing things down in a journal. Once I started writing things down, I could keep track of what I had to do much better, along with peeking at any deadlines or graduation requirements I had not met, such as senior dues as well as turning in all of my community service hours. College applications were a small obstacle, but I had started on the majority of them early on in the year before I really started getting busy. My mother, grandmother, and I came together through all of the stress. We helped each other take it one step at a time. The three of us working together as a unit and a family is the primary reason I was able to work on my time management and balance everything, thus not missing any deadlines.

If I could go back, I would have started writing things in a journal as early as middle school. This would have made it second nature, and I would not have missed out on some great opportunities. Writing things down has been even more effective for me than making reminders in my iPhone, and I now take my book almost everywhere I go. Another thing I would do is communicate better with my family and my counselors. There are many deadlines I missed or came fearfully close to missing due to keeping things to myself. I nearly did not graduate, and also came close to not getting FAFSA and DC TAG from poor communication. Luckily, I didn't miss these deadlines. I learned that communication is necessary and will pay off and carry over while in college and when I get full-time employment or start my own business.

# Relationships: with Teachers, Guidance Counselors, Employers, and Parents

The positive connections that any of us make with the people around us are critical to leading a fulfilling and meaningful life. Treating the adults in your life with kindness and respect will make it easy for them to offer you the same consideration.

Remember that your teachers are there to help you, so when they have office hours or offer up free time for students to visit and ask questions, take advantage of it. Even if you do not have a specific burning question, getting to know your teachers and guidance counselors will definitely help you through high school and the college application process.

*I spent a decent amount of my high school career stressing about classes and school-work, but along the way I made many connections. When it comes time to start applying to colleges of their choice, students potentially need recommendation letters from teachers or administrators to be sent out with their applications. It is hard to get a recommendation letter from a teacher who knows nothing about you, so I believe it is important to start making teacher-connections as soon as possible.*

—LANAE BARROW, BOWLING GREEN STATE UNIVERSITY

The same advice goes for your employers, coaches, mentors, family members, and friends. Relationships matter. Take care of them. And don't forget to thank the people who are on your team for their support.

## Work on Those Soft Skills

The skills you develop by nurturing your interpersonal connections will be just as important in college and career. According to Tia McNair, vice president for the Office of Diversity, Equity, and Student Success at the Association of American Colleges and Universities (AAC&U), "Colleges and universities are intentionally trying to help develop proficiencies in teamwork, problem solving skills, critical thinking and communication skills, quantitative reasoning, ethical reasoning skills." She urges students in high school to take advantage of those opportunities to get out in the community or join a team to develop those valuable skills.

Torrence Traynham advises, "Appreciate the team and collaborative projects that your teachers and professors assign to you. Between now and your early career years, you'll find yourself engaging in dozens of collaborative projects. I was the kind of student who didn't like to collaborate. I'm a Type 'A' personality; I like things done a certain way and figured I could do things on my own. But that just isn't the way it works in the real world."

Those skills like teamwork, collaboration, communication, leadership, critical thinking, and problem solving are often referred to as "soft skills," which are highly regarded by university presidents and corporate executives alike. Oglethorpe University President Larry Schall states, "Soft skills are critical. The students that I see who are the most successful, whether they are coming out of Oglethorpe or Harvard, are the ones who can sit down and have a conversation with you; they can write a letter. If you give them a problem they can figure out a way to solve it—whether that's teaming up with someone, finding someone else to help, doing research, or getting advice. They aren't fearful. They've made some mistakes in their life and have learned from them."

Christine Krull, director of diversity and inclusion at Roche Diagnostics adds, "Soft skills are where students can set themselves apart. Colleges and employers are looking for individuals who can communicate, who have leadership skills, who are about collaborating and bringing people together. Take advantage of opportunities to develop those skills. Put yourself out there and take some risks. That's how we all learn and get better."

You may be hyper-focused on the math problems you need to solve for an upcoming test or the history facts you'll be asked to recite in a paper due next week, but those hard facts and figures may not be the ones that will elevate you in your future. Alan Nevel, senior vice president, chief diversity and human resources officer for The MetroHealth System says, "When I look for a new employee, I look for those soft skills. I can teach you the hard skills. I also look for people with a diverse set of experiences. Make sure you take credit for the things you are doing now. If you are leading a club or non-profit organization in high school, you are a CEO."

# Polish Your Image

That step from high school to college is a big one. Right around the same time, you will also be making the transition from child to adult. With that new status in life will come a different level of expectations and responsibility. It's time to stand a little straighter and taller, make eye contact, and master a friendly greeting that includes a firm handshake. Trust me. This one simple exchange can mean the difference between a good first impression or not.

Go ahead and practice it; right now!! Walk into a room with an unfamiliar face, reach out your hand, look the person in the eye with a smile and say, "Hi, my name is <Jim>. It's a pleasure to meet you." If that seems too scary or awkward, try it with friends or your parents first until it feels more natural. You will need this skill when you visit campuses and if your application involves an interview with an admissions representative.

You should scrub your digital presence as well. That means making sure your email address is proper and professional and your social media accounts don't contain any inappropriate or embarrassing posts. An inappropriate email address can reveal more than a carefully edited essay. That email address lazyboy16@idontcare.com might have seemed funny in eighth grade, but it does not work for college applications. Colleges have been known to revoke acceptances if they discover inappropriate online social media posts. Universities take their reputations very seriously and expect their students to reflect these standards. Even if you skirt past the college admissions process with a less than honorable social media presence, future employers or potential employers, and even the public may call you out. Two professional baseball players had to make public apologies when someone dug into their past posts (from their teenage years) and found some unsavory tweets. A career or a college opportunity can be ruined in 140 characters or less. A good rule of thumb is to only post things that you would be proud to show your grandmother.

# Don't Worry, Be Happy

If all of this advice is just adding to your already long to-do list and making you even more stressed and anxious, try to take a step back and put it all in perspective. It may be hard, or even impossible, for you to get out from under the looming deadlines, tests, and checklists, but more than a few of the students we hear from regularly wish that they had lightened up a bit and enjoyed the ride more.

*If I have to offer one piece of advice, it would be to not take college applications too seriously. Growing up, high school, it should be fun. Getting into college is not the finish line of your life journey. And you will not ultimately become successful just because you have gotten into a prestigious university. It is who you are and how you make the most out of your existing circumstances that matters the most. The whole purpose of the college application process, I believe, is to help you find your passion, allowing you to know more about yourself.*

—ALISON SIN, CORNELL UNIVERSITY
(INTERNATIONAL STUDENT FROM HONG KONG;
ACCEPTED EARLY DECISION)

Granted, it's a lot easier to look back and advise others to enjoy more and stress less when you have already landed a spot at a great school, but really, we hear it over and over again.

*My one overriding piece of advice is to enjoy your last year of high school, because you will only get to experience it once. Do not let the stress of applications or any rejection letters take away from your senior year. On that note, though, also enjoy the process of transitioning to your next journey in life. Always follow your heart and go with your gut feeling when it comes to deciding where to go to college.*

—SHANAYA SIDHU, UCLA

# Just Breathe

In the musical, *In the Heights*, by Lin-Manuel Miranda, the main character Nina sings a song called "Breathe." She has just returned to her neighborhood after losing her scholarship at Stanford. She feels like a failure. "The biggest disappointment you know," she sings. The song is a pep talk to herself to straighten her spine, face her friends and family, and just breathe.

There are likely to be setbacks, small hiccups, and even spectacular failures along the way. It is normal. And no matter how perfect everyone else's path appears to be on the surface, people's public personas are not a true gauge of reality. Know that even top students, star athletes, and school leaders have ups and downs.

When things get tough and you stumble, be kind to yourself. Don't forget to take care of basic needs…like eating, sleeping, exercising, and staying healthy. That advice also goes for the times when you are on a roll. No matter how busy you think you are, you have time to take a five-minute break to take deep breaths and eat a snack or drink some water. Remember you are human, and though you are certainly ready to take on life at a competitive college and the world beyond, a little yoga and an early night's rest is often exactly what you need to have a successful high school experience. Taking care of yourself physically can seriously improve your mental abilities. Sleeping the recommended amount, eating healthy, and exercising can all help boost your brain power and get you through the day, week, semester, and year on a high note. Intense stress and all-nighters are not the way to improve your GPA.

*While you might be stressed about getting into college, remember that if you put in the effort and time, you will see results. And don't forget to take time to breathe and enjoy your senior (or junior, sophomore…) year, you'll only experience it once! I didn't know what my dream school was when I applied, but now that I have committed, I am confident I ended up in the perfect place for me.*

—ARIF HARIANAWALA, UNIVERSITY OF TEXAS AT AUSTIN

Larry Schall, president of Oglethorpe University says, "There is an incredible amount of pressure on students.... Some of the pressure is parental; some of it comes from inside the student. And students have a sense that since they have been working so hard since kindergarten to get to college, that they want to be rewarded for all that work." The trick is to manage those expectations and not get too hung up on the idea of one result, one school, one right way to proceed. Pat yourself on the back for accomplishments, but don't beat yourself up if you don't achieve what you'd hoped. Those dips, falters, fumbles, and failures will make you stronger in the end.

# Consider a Gap Year or Semester

You don't have to set out with the idea of taking a semester or yearlong break before starting college, but keep it in the back of your mind as an option in case it makes sense for you. I've heard of students who were so exhausted and burned out from pushing themselves in high school that they needed a break to recharge and reignite their passion for learning. Schools will often let you defer your acceptance for a year if you communicate with them within a specified timeframe. Some even strongly encourage it. A gap year can also help your chance at admission to more competitive colleges as it gives you the opportunity to explore your interests and passions with more depth and strengthen your college admission application.

In an article published on Harvard's website entitled "Time Out or Burn Out for the Next Generation" the authors (William Fitzsimmons, Dean of Admission & Financial Aid, Harvard College; Marlyn E. McGrath, Director of Admissions, Harvard College; and Charles Ducey, Adjunct Lecturer in Psychology, Harvard Graduate School of Education) write, "For nearly four decades, Harvard has recommended [students] take a year off before college, indeed proposing it in the letter of admissions...The results have been uniformly positive."

Some schools will even offer spring admission to a deserving student who applied for fall but for whom they didn't have a spot. This "February Freshman" path is not as common and rarely advertised by schools, but I've heard families of students who take these offers refer to them as gifts. Students do a lot of maturing and grow huge amounts of self-awareness in those few months before starting college in the spring. Plus, they say that they avoided a lot of the first-semester freshman silliness that sometimes happens when large groups of teenagers land on campus with newfound freedom. Everyone is a bit more grounded come spring.

What you do with that bonus semester or year is entirely up to you and your circumstances. Get a job or internship, visit relatives in another part of the country, volunteer for a cause, help care for a relative, or simply go out and experience the world.

Education and learning are important, but learning does not just have to occur in an academic setting. While academic learning gives you the power to understand the complexities of the world better and make more informed decisions as an individual and global citizen, learning that occurs outside the classroom lends power in a different form. Learning from your mistakes and learning to be independent empower you to grow and develop your own set of personal values and beliefs. Learning in any form is an adventure.

*I applied for the spring semester on somewhat of a hunch that it would be easier to get in since fewer high school seniors would be applying at that time. I heard back only 2 or 3 days later that I had been accepted for the 2018 spring semester at LCAD.*

—PHOENIX ROSE HOFFMAN,
LAGUNA COLLEGE OF ART AND DESIGN (LCAD)

There are a number of well-run organizations that can help organize a gap year or semester abroad if you can raise the money. There are also excellent gap year programs offered domestically through some universities. According to the Gap Year Association, "Taking a structured gap year invariably serves to develop the individual into a more focused student with a better sense of purpose and engagement in the world." Studies have shown that students who take a gap year perform better academically once at college. They can also be better community members, better at working in groups, more clear about their academic and career goals, and more employable. The experience of living in a different culture or stepping outside of your comfort zone can have a profoundly positive impact on your personal development and sense of self. Remember those soft skills mentioned a few pages back? They will improve too.

Some parents worry that if their child takes time off after high school that he or she will never go to college. The statistics prove otherwise, however. About 90% of the students who take a gap return to college within a year and are often better prepared for success.

# Are You Ready for Early College?

Perhaps you are one of those people who is always a few steps ahead when talking (or walking) with a group. Maybe you feel as if you have absorbed all you can from your current school environment. Or you have been thinking about and planning for college for so long that you want to get that show on the road sooner, rather than later. Some people just can't wait. Still others have failed to thrive or meet their full potential in their traditional high school setting. The good news is that there are ways to accelerate your path to and through college if you are motivated.

Many public school systems have early college high school or dual-enrollment programs that allow students to earn their high school diploma while also enrolling in courses for college credit. This can be a smart way to enter college with a load of credits. You just need to be aware that some credits may not transfer. And sometimes receiving too many university credits during high school can actually be detrimental for college admissions. At the University of California, for example, a high school student who receives a few college credits during high school would then be considered a "transfer student" and would be competing against the community college transfer students who have taken a specific track of two years of coursework. You should talk to your career counselor or the admissions advisors at the universities where you want to apply prior to taking university course credits during the academic year.

NATALIE CHANDLER,
BAYLOR UNIVERSITY

I took many dual credit classes and will be entering freshman year in the fall with 22 credits. I personally prefer dual credit classes, specifically online, because I like the dual credit system better than the AP system. I have friends who are in AP and some love it but some hate it. Ultimately it comes down to personal preference. I compared the pros and cons of each and talked to friends who had done both to get their input before making my decision. I loved taking dual credit classes online because it isn't a class full of high school students taught by a high school teacher. It is a college class taught by a professor, and the online aspect allows for many different kinds of people to be in the class which makes the learning experience more insightful when different ethnicities, generations, and personalities are all in one class. In my politics class, there were a few high school seniors all the way to a 40-something-year-old mom who was going back to get her degree. Discussions were so interesting as it was not just teenagers represented in the classes. There were all kinds of people with different experiences and lives represented. It adds to the class and makes it more than just learning the material; you learn more about people and their beliefs, which is the most interesting part I think. Ultimately it is personal preference: online or traditional, dual credit or AP. Taking dual credit classes was something I knew I wanted to do by sophomore year. I started them senior year and while I wish I started junior year, I have achieved many credits and will save so much money. I am even taking dual credit classes this summer. It's only two classes but after this summer, I will only have one semester of math and one semester of history left of my core classes. That's what one should be focused on taking: core classes. English, history, electives, math and sometimes science are all core classes that are usually required for every major. Getting a major course plan from your university can help decide which classes to take now before college. I found my major's degree plan and I figured out I will enter the fall as a second semester freshman and I am just a few credits from being a sophomore.

Another "early college" route is enrolling in a four-year institution at a young age. At a school like Bard College at Simon's Rock in Massachusetts, you can actually leave high school in tenth or eleventh grade without a diploma (or standardized test results) to start college. Everyone at Simon's Rock begins college early, so students are surrounded by their peers and supported by faculty and staff in a rigorous BA program specifically designed for younger scholars.

*I always loved being independent, whether it was on projects or just to take care of myself. To be in a place where I can do exactly that, further my education, and be able to do it at the age of sixteen is one of the best things imaginable for me. The ability to advance my career and be able to grow as a person are just a few of the reasons I am excited to become part of the community at Bard College at Simon's Rock.*

—GARRISON FUNK, BARD COLLEGE AT SIMON'S ROCK

These less traditional options are a way to bypass a high school education system that, at times, is more about promoting students through a series of mandated requirements than promoting their love of learning. Dr. Ian Bickford, the provost at Simon's Rock and an alumnus of the school himself says, "high school students today spend an increasing proportion of their time thinking about getting into college. Yet applying to college tells students next to nothing about what to expect there. High school, conventionally conceived, does not prepare students for college. At best it prepares students *to apply* to college."

Creating early-access bridges from high school to college can serve as an equalizer. Dr. Bickford says, "Even in this promising age of inclusion and equity on college campuses, the high-school-to-college gatekeeping system overwhelmingly benefits the elite and the affluent. The Early College model is about more than acceleration to college. It addresses inequities across secondary and higher education, with significant implications for who has access to college, when, and at what cost."

It's not for everyone, but the students who choose early college are often looking for something more than they are getting from their local high school. "Students who start college early bring an energy and a capacity to their learning, undisturbed by the frustrations of the last years of high school," says Bickford. Here is one student's application essay, describing why she wanted to start college early at Simon's Rock.

### WHY HERE, WHY NOW

ELLIE ROSTAN,
BARD COLLEGE AT SIMON'S ROCK

Let me begin with this: as years pass, limbs grow and clothes shrink. But there is still sentimental fondness to threadbare things, only salvageable with patches and nets of stitches. A hole appears there, in the thinning denim of diminishing pant leg. Then there is another, almost hiding on the hem of your favorite skirt. Years pass and new patches are applied—until pants and skirts are strung together with ever loosening webs of thread and you cannot get away with another day, of wearing your best-loved skirt. And yet, you try to make it work. Not facing the fact that it is time to throw them away. It is time to buy new clothes and with that time, fond memories will be cultivated. And you will be glad.

Analogies can only be stretched so far, but I think this one fits perfectly on my laptop screen—where this essay is being composed. So let's rewind to elementary school where my clothes are faultlessly intact. Forward now to junior high: the period of time when somehow, my clothes have begun to fall apart. One by one, pieces of fabrics dislodge themselves and drop to the linoleum floor. Let us watch as I try to pick them all up, as I anxiously—almost sweating now, piece my pants and my favorite skirt back together again. More patches are applied, though I feel as if all hope has been lost.

Public school has a way of extracting the love of learning, curiosity, and scholarly illuminations, from the heart of an adolescent girl. There I was—stranded in a jam-packed hallway, clothes being yanked from me. The thing that provided me with safety and necessity torn away so violently. And no one seemed to notice except for me. Teachers droned, memorization encouraged. I even wrote a poem expanding on my repulsion of the boredom and monotony that seemed to radiate from cinder block corners.

When high school arrived, I left monotony behind and entered a small private school. Oh! How good it felt to be rejuvenated again. As if air was being pumped back into my lungs. I had finally bought new clothes, and I smelled the sweet smell of laundry detergent. Projects and essays knocked politely on the door of my brain and I welcomed them with a smile that could have split my face in two. That's how wide it was. And yet, there was a nag at the back of my mind. However slight, I noticed it. Noticed more and more as it grew. Because with a small school, comes limitations, and I do not like to be held back.

That is why I am sitting here, essay unfurling itself languidly on the once blank page of my computer screen. I want to be challenged, surrounded by people who think like me and don't complain about the prospects of learning. Because learning is a gift! It is a delicacy that should be savored by the young and the old alike. Learning is a new pair of pants or a skirt that will be loved and won't fall apart. I believe that Bard at Simon's Rock will be this gift. Bard at Simon's Rock will not hold me back.

Yes. "Learning is a gift," and some students want to engage in a deeper discourse with college-level professors who are experts in their fields sooner, rather than later. An accelerated track for highly motivated students can help you reach your high school, college, and career goals ahead of your peers.

*I decided I would graduate high school in three years instead of four. As a result, I was never on the traditional schedule. When you are trying to complete high school in three-fourths of the time you have to create your own schedule. I had to navigate college at a different pace than my age mates, to catch up with my fellow graduates. I was genuinely taking the college courses alongside my high school courses so that I could achieve my goal of graduating high school early. However, I do feel like they prepared me academically for college. I took my classes at a local community college; as a result I had the opportunity to taste the college life just a little bit.*

—Eyram Akakpo, University of Akron (education dual major)

# Community College as a Bridge to Your Dream

There are many benefits to starting your college journey at a community college and then transferring to a four-year university once you have a year or two of credits in hand. This is a route is underutilized and, for whatever reason, underappreciated. Students who go to community college first end up with the same four-year degree as those who start at a four-year college, and they save A LOT of money. It's also a great option for students who may not yet feel fully prepared for university or want more time to choose their "dream school."

### How I Got Into My Dream School

Bethany Greenwood,
Florida State University

It was always my dream to join the Seminoles and live by the rules of vires, artes, mores. I started thinking about college around tenth grade when others would ask me about it. I already knew that I wanted to go to Florida State University because of all the stories my mother told me about her experience. Getting into university was not going to be easy so I started working harder to improve my chances. I got ahead in high school by dual enrolling in the community college in my town, North Florida Community College. Some of the courses I took this way counted for high school credits and college credits. I was ahead of other students in my class and could take more college classes the closer I got to graduation. During this time, I had already been looking at certain majors for FSU and looking at the different prerequisites for each one. The clubs I was involved in had even taken trips to different colleges. I also searched for scholarships that could help with my transition. Because I was dual enrolling, the courses I was taking at NFCC were paid for by my high school, so I had no idea of how much college would cost. Dealing with college and high school courses was a difficult schedule. I had to make sure none of my classes overlapped and that I had transportation to get there on time. The courses were overwhelming since I was not used to the shift in the curriculum and expectations of my professors. The homework was plentiful and more difficult than I was expecting, but as graduation moved closer I worked harder.

However, once I graduated high school I wasn't quite ready for life in a university setting. I had to look for other options to prepare myself for the next stage of my education. So, I made a pit stop, and became an eagle at Tallahassee Community College. I took courses there for a year, finishing my AA degree while also knocking out some of my prerequisites for my intended major. My courses from dual enrollment helped me to jump ahead once I started at TCC. Plus with my experience at NFCC, the transition was a bit easier than I expected. The crossover from community college to university was a scary one but I was glad I made the choice.

Tallahassee Community College was a typical small-town college with a surprising amount of spirit. The professors were always ready to help a struggling student. One of my first classes was College Success, a course intended to help new students adjust to college life. The course material consisted of different ways to improve skills like time management, prioritizing, and studying. In addition to that, many of our assignments were to help us in learning what resources were available on campus. My intended major for FSU was psychology, so I had to make sure that my schedule was tailored not only to finish my AA degree but to also complete prerequisites for the program.

The resources were everywhere, and the most important rule was to utilize all of them. I would even ask my professors about their experience in college and how they dealt with everything. The departments of the school would always send emails reminding me of resources and different opportunities on campus. The advising center was a big help, not only because they were involved in helping choose classes, but because they also held things like job fairs and advisement fairs. These fairs would include advisors from different colleges along with the TCC advisors. The FSU advisors were always split up by departments, so I would meet with the human sciences or applied sciences advisor. Through the month, I would go through my courses, meet with my regular advisor, then meet with an FSU advisor to make sure I was on track for both my AA degree and transition into university.

The biggest resource to help me into FSU was the special programs that TCC had for their students. The first program that I was taken into was the 2+2 program, which went into effect once I was accepted into TCC. In the state of Florida, individuals who earn an Associate in Arts degree at a community college in the state are guaranteed admission to one of the partnering universities to the program. Because my goal was to earn an AA degree during my time at TCC, I was already guaranteed a spot at FSU. This was only for the general admission so I still had to apply for my intended major. The next program that I was taken into was the TCC2FSU program. The program is very similar to 2+2, but it came with extra benefits. It included transfer-focused advisors from both colleges and even supported students applying for limited access programs. I was applying for general admission into FSU and admission into the psychology program, one of the university's limited access programs. These programs played a huge part in my admission into FSU and changed the way I would have to transfer to university.

Once I started the application process to FSU, it immediately took a turn from the normal application process. My first step was to complete the general application for FSU and then the psychology program application. I was also required to send information such as transcripts, my FAFSA application, and different insurance records. I was not, however, required to write an application essay. With the programs I was in, my spot was already guaranteed so an essay was not necessary. Because I was a transfer student my orientation for FSU was also different. Usually it consists of a two-day stay on campus in one of the dorm halls, but I was only required to stay for a few hours. Orientation consisted of a small tour of the campus, different seminars to explore the resources on campus, and our first advisor meeting to meet the advisors and students of the program and create our schedule for the semester. I had already been to the campus before on field trips but this was a different experience. It was very immersive and a bit overwhelming because of how much information I was learning.

# Creating Your List of Schools

Building a list of colleges and universities that you are interested in is an ongoing process that requires you to constantly reflect, reach out, and refine. Reflect inward to define what you want; reach out to collect information; and refine the list as you learn more about yourself and your options. "Start with the experience that you want, not with the name of the school," says Emily Pacheco, Outreach and Admissions Specialist, International Programs, UC Berkeley Extension.

*Around midway through the second half of junior year, it is a good idea to talk to your parents about college if you have not yet done so. Establishing who will be paying for college, where they expect you to stay geographically, and discussing potential career paths can ease all parties involved. This will then give you the foundation to begin researching, visiting, and applying to schools.*

—ARIF HARIANAWALA, UNIVERSITY OF TEXAS AT AUSTIN

# Reflect

Know yourself and define your preferences.

When you envision your future, what do you see? When you picture yourself at college, how does it look? Figuring out what you want from a school requires you to look inward first. Analyze your true intentions. Why do you actually want to go to college? It shouldn't be simply because everyone around you expects you to. Once you begin to analyze your intrinsic motivations towards college, you will be able to discover your true values and passions and true college fit. Here are a few basic criteria to think about:

> **Size**—Do you want a small school with more personal attention or a large university where you can blend into the crowd?

> **Location**—How far from home do you want to be? Are you looking for an urban or more rural setting?

> **Public or Private**

> **Campus Setting**—Urban and hip? Or rural and bucolic?

> **Cost**—How much debt are you willing to take on and how much are your parents willing and able to contribute?

> **Your Major**—Look at department-level ranking. A university ranked lower overall may have a top department in your desired major.

> **Learning Environment**—highly competitive? Nurturing? Small classes?

## Studying vs. Social Life?

These factors will vary based on your situation, but as you look at different schools be sure to highlight any "make or break" criteria that you notice. Are you only interested in co-ed schools? Do the Historically Black Colleges and Universities (HBCUs) hold special appeal? Is a Division 1 athletic program important to you?

*I found my dream school by researching as much as possible about potential schools I was interested in. I looked at prices of tuition, room and board, meal plans, what housing they had, student activities and life, and their traditions. It is important to look at what student life is like and what organizations they have on campus for you. Knowing where you would want to live, the clubs you would join, and the traditions you could embrace can help you imagine yourself there. Out of the many schools I applied to, I only was really interested in two: Baylor University and Texas A&M University. These were also the only two colleges I had actually been to. When looking at schools, I feel it is important to know what you want and what kind of experience. Ask yourself "Do I want to go to a large university or a small one? Is private or public right for me? What kind of hobbies do I enjoy and are those available in or around campus?" I knew that the town/area my college was in was important to me. I wanted to feel at home and have a small town feel but with lots to still do. When visiting campus, keep these things in mind when walking around and exploring outside of campus. Get to know the city or town and what there is to do. Take advantage of free tours and go during the summer or breaks to walk around by yourself and try to imagine you living there. I knew that Baylor would be the best place for me to be and where I would succeed. I knew the moment I stepped on campus the first time and explored Waco. I fell in love with not only the campus but the entire town. I knew it was where I wanted to be for the next chapter my life and even the next few chapters after college.*

—NATALIE CHANDLER, BAYLOR UNIVERSITY

"Students often pick a dream school that is on everybody's dream school list, like Harvard, Stanford, or Yale. At other times, students are drawn to a hot school that everyone is talking about. And in some states, there are flagship public institutions like the University of Georgia which has gotten really competitive and quite hard to get into," says Larry Schall, president of Oglethorpe University. "I spend a lot of time with high school students and I ask them what they want from college. Choosing a school is one of the biggest decisions they will make, and that can feel daunting. But I stress to them that there is no single perfect school for every student. There are many good options for everyone." The important thing is to identify the kind of school that will work best for you. Schall adds, "Students are different. Some thrive in really competitive environments, others need something a bit less stressful."

## Do Your Research

The BigFuture.CollegeBoard.org website has a tool to help you start your research. It walks you through your answers to some of these questions to help you narrow down the field. It also has answers to basic questions like, "What does liberal arts mean?" and "What's the difference between a university and a college?" MyOptions. org, created by ACT and the National Research Center for College and University Admission (NRCCUA), is another tool that incorporates preference quizzes to help you identify good school matches. The app also offers free lessons filled with advice about the application process. Set aside some time to page through the resources on these sites and others as you figure out the qualities that are important to you. You will end up with a snapshot that will serve as a good starting point and a way to eliminate some of the sea of choices that the nearly 5,000 colleges and universities in the U.S. offer.

When researching schools, look for institutions that not only offer the basics but that align with your interests. What do you dream about and love to learn and think about in your spare time? What schools seem to highlight those things? But if you aren't exactly sure what you want to study, don't worry. Understanding your true desires isn't always obvious. It can emerge over time.

*Early in your high school career, pick three random colleges, and compare them. Perhaps try an elite school, and state school, and one you might be mildly interested in, or any combination of universities that pique your interest. For each school, research admissions requirements, cost of attendance and financial aid information, and even old essay prompts, if you can find them, as well as student access to resources like professors or lab positions. This exercise serves as a good introduction to what universities are looking for in their applicants, and doing this early allows you to prepare for challenging classes later, or plan for what standardized tests you'll need to take. This also allows you to start thinking about what qualities you'll look for in universities you'll apply to, such as the size of the student body, the student to faculty ratio, and emphasis placed on undergraduate learning as opposed to graduate student learning. Such research is especially helpful if you're not sure yet what you want to study. Having said that, once you have an idea of what you want to study, you can narrow down your college options by applying to schools that specialize in your area. Don't worry about changing your mind though; at most schools, you don't have to declare your major until your sophomore year.*

—MAILE HARRIS, YALE UNIVERSITY,
(NSHSS AMBASSADOR)

One of our scholarship finalists tells a story of how his true passion was hiding in plain sight. Thankfully, he realized it at the last minute and followed his gut.

JARON CHALIER,
CARLETON UNIVERSITY, CANADA

HOW I GOT INTO MY DREAM SCHOOL
BY STARTING OVER

Do you know what you want to do with the rest of your life? Did you think you will know what you want to do with the rest of your life when you are applying to universities—a decision that will affect the next four years of your life and your future career? I did. I had an epiphany that came from a healthy dose of introspection a month before university deadlines, meaning I completely redid my university plans from scratch after already doing the background research, application essays, personal information, and paying the application fees for seven universities. I could not be happier with my decision and thank myself every time I think about it, because I got into my dream school, and I'd like to share my experience to help others make incredible life choices too.

For years, I had always wanted to be a mechanical engineer, so I could be an inventor. It always appealed to me as a kid, since I had a vision of inventing groundbreaking technology of different kinds and in areas other than mechanical engineering. I had my ideals based on a child's view of the world, thinking about what seemed cool and not what is actually possible. For example, I thought about inventing a new way of harvesting renewable energy that would singularly lead to the end of needing coal and oil. I thought about making something from *Star Wars* work in real life, like a light saber. I wanted to make something from *Willy Wonka's Chocolate Factory* work in real life, like a chocolate bird that can chirp and flap its wings, or an ice cream that wouldn't melt even on a hot day. To achieve these adorable goals, I even tried to get ahead of things in middle school by attempting to read through *Mechanical Engineering for Dummies* at my public library. I realized pretty quickly that I couldn't understand calculus as a 12-year old as I am no prodigy. It took me another year or two before I got out of my dazzling visions of making the tools and gadgets of science fiction movies a reality, but I still wanted to be an engineer.

Working towards this goal of mine, I took science classes and went to two engineering summer camps. I took AP physics, Chemistry, and AP Calculus. I got decent grades, though I always did the bare minimum since I loathed math homework and had trouble focusing in class. At the summer camps, I had fun while learning about engineering and exploring possibilities for university. These factored into ignoring what I genuinely cared about and enjoyed, since I was doing just fine and didn't see anything wrong with my path.

Another class I took in high school was AP Comparative Government, which has nothing to do with engineering. While I was happy to read about the recent political history of several countries and discuss the effects of their different policies, I struggled to learn about derivatives and how to use different formulas. I enjoyed fighting an uphill battle where I was given a pro-Putin side in a class debate on whether Putin is right to lead Russia but didn't do anything in the way of building some kind of device for practicing mechanical engineering. I gladly kept up on the current events of each country we looked at in each class, but stopped my subscription to a monthly science magazine because I never read it. My teachers and friends who knew me saw that while I was focused on science, I enjoyed talking about culture, modern politics, and language, but they also didn't feel the need to try to steer me in another direction. All these things happened over time, and I ignored and overlooked all of them.

I went to a summer camp at an engineering college in Boston for several weeks, also visiting MIT in the process since it's a world-famous engineering school, and I also went to Canada's top engineering school, the University of Waterloo, for several weeks the following summer. When I went to visit MIT, I decided universities that are top-notch by reputation weren't going to be my top choices just because of their status. While graduates and employees of MIT have done incredible things and are all certainly intelligent, I found that it was not the university for me. I wasn't likely to receive a scholarship since my grades and SAT scores weren't high enough, and I also detested the campus because it felt more like a tourist zone than a place for learning, considering all of the plaques everywhere and all of the people coming in and out. I decided that a small college like the one I was staying at in Boston wasn't for me since I would be around a similar group of people for a long time. I then decided that studying in the U.S. wasn't even for me from learning more about the reputation for high fees and extremely high student debt. I decided to use my Canadian citizenship to look into schools there, and was pleasantly surprised about how out-of-province fees as a citizen are lower than in-state fees for a U.S. citizen.

As can be seen quite clearly, I had devoted my years growing up, my class choices, my summers, my free time, my university research, my part-time jobs, my summer camps, and on and on, all towards an idea of pursuing mechanical engineering. By mid-December, I sat waiting for acceptances and rejections. The first thing I received was a rejection from a university. This forced me to sit down and think hard about my abilities, my grades, my applications, everything.

As I sat there in an awful state, because a university decided to reject me at the earliest possible time, even though I was still waiting on around six other universities, I thought back to my interest in languages despite not being fluent in more than one. I thought back to how my classmates told me I should take this one economics course since it related to me by addressing politics and being based on real life and not solely theory. I thought back to when I was in elementary school, and all embellishment aside, I did used to sit and stare at maps for long periods of time—it's just what interested me. All that thinking during who knows how many minutes as I sat staring at my rejection email in my living room, led me to the conclusion that I would be incredibly more suited to something more like politics rather than mechanical engineering.

I talked to my two closest friends about it, I talked to my mom and my sister about it, I talked to a teacher about it, and they all basically agreed that that's who I was. I was amazed, noticing how every single person I talked to agreed that it really did seem like a snug fit for me to go into something like that. So, what I ended up deciding on was international relations. About three or four days after everything I had just gone through, I completely ditched it. I completely. Ditched it. I started researching universities relating to politics in Canada.

I knew I wanted a good, generally respected education. I wanted to be in a proper-sized city, in a medium to large university. I needed one that could offer me scholarships and/or cheap tuition. Lastly, I would prefer to be in the capital because that's where the seat of the government and embassies are, making logical sense for my program to network, find internships, find scholarships, etc. That's what led me to applying to Carleton University. It's a solid education, being renowned mainly for its graduate program as it was in the top two with Harvard in one review that a professor mentioned. It's in a city, although a small one, and it's a medium-sized enrollment. I was offered a scholarship with my acceptance, and I have cheaper tuition even not being from that province, because out-of-province tuition is still cheaper than in-state tuition in most U.S. states. Even more to my excitement, they publicly advertised their "capital advantage" that earns university students internships on Parliament Hill, where the equivalent of the American House and Senate sit. There is a club that organizes embassy visits, and the university hosts many foreign and Canadian ambassadors to give talks on campus. It seemed already an amazing fit, but then I also noticed that they were starting a new type of international relations program.

It also incorporated a mandatory foreign language fluency require-ment, mandatory overseas experience, and classes like global history that contrast with other programs/universities doing Canadian history instead. It made me confident even though it was a recently created program. It became my best fit and top choice university and I got in with a scholarship, making me feel like Carleton fit me and I fit it.

My overriding and genuinely indispensable advice to those still in high school is to be absolutely sure to know about yourself and the work you'd like to do by taking the time to sit down and think ahead. This could be especially difficult for many cultures where often it's the country's top three universities or bust, as often the job culture is privilege and priority for graduates of name-brand universities. What people need to keep in mind is if you deliberately get yourself into a situation that will not leave you comfortable or happy the entire time, which in turn will make you unhappy with your life and affect your studies.

Now as my first year has finished, I am happy, proud, and have found my passion in life and I want everyone else to feel like I do. Take to heart to what I've written and sit down and think about yourself, which leads to thinking about what you will do after high school, which leads to thinking about your career.

Once you have at least an inkling of an idea of the kinds of schools you are interested in, make a list. At this point the list can be longer than you ultimately want, but try to keep it to no more than 15 or 20 schools.

# Reach Out

Talk to counselors, go on visits and interviews, research online, and request informational brochures. College websites are a good place to start. Take the time to explore them thoroughly, as you could find information that could help you decide whether or not a school is right for you. The information on their sites can also make the application process easier. Also, connecting to schools through social media can help give you a better "on the ground" picture of a university and can provide current student perspectives that you may not find on college websites.

*Accumulate as much information as you can when making this important, informed decision. Contact current students, visit campuses, research on websites and student forums, and talk to the college itself. You have so many avenues of information, so go out there and learn as much as you can.*

—Shanaya Sidhu, UCLA

While some experts recommend visiting as many schools as you can, Larry Schall, president of Oglethorpe University, cautions families not to try to pack in too many short tours. It's better to spend an overnight or sit in on a class at a select few schools so you can absorb the school culture. He says, "schools can look alike on the surface, but every school has its own culture which comes up from the students. The longer you can experience a place by going to the dining hall and talking to people on campus, the better you can understand that student-grown culture."

Families sometimes consider waiting to visit schools until after you have been accepted. "The problem with waiting is that some schools are now weighing demonstrated interest in their school when evaluating applications, and interest can be gauged by whether or not you have visited or have shown your enthusiasm for the institution in some other way," says Nancy Beane, who has been a college counselor for 27 years and is the former president of the National Association of College Admissions Counselors. "If you don't have the resources to visit a school that is high on your list, send a note or email to the admissions person in your area. Let them know that you haven't been able to visit but you have interest in the school."

Kimberly Tyson, USA Liaison Officer at the University of Alberta in Canada agrees. "Connecting with your first-choice college is critical. It shows initiative and that you are interested in taking next steps. Get connected via social media or the university's website to stay updated on university news and campus events including recruitment events for prospective students. Attending recruitment events/college fairs or visiting the campus in-person, gives students an opportunity to ask questions in a face-to-face environment, gain a better understanding of the admissions process, and academic programs available. Some colleges may also waive application fees during recruitment events which can help save students money."

Many colleges will set up regional information sessions in major cities around the country if you can't make it to their campus. Keep in mind that these sessions are intended to show off the best qualities of the school and are often in large event-space conference rooms so it may be hard to get a feel for the culture of a school this way. The best way to get a feel for a school is to attend classes, talk to current students, and do an overnight in a dorm, if possible.

ESTHER BEDOYAN,
CARNEGIE MELLON UNIVERSITY

I visited Carnegie Mellon twice; once during the summer for an interview with a college admissions counselor who later happened to be my regional counselor as well, and a second time in the fall where I stayed overnight and attended classes, information sessions, and visited their dormitories. I felt that the second visit was significant because it gave me a more accurate understanding of the school and it solidified my decision to apply Early Decision. By researching CMU's engineering programs online prior to my first visit, I found that it offered a dual major program, where Biomedical Engineering was specifically designed to be taken only as an additional major to a traditional engineering major, such as Electrical and Computer Engineering (ECE). I also communicated by email and Skype and later met with in person some BME and ECE professors who were very helpful with answering any remaining questions that I had about their respective programs at CMU. I also met and spoke with two CMU students who were BME dual majors and inquired about their academic workload, career development experiences, and overall college experiences. I met my regional admissions counselor again at a regional information session hosted at a local school near my city.

The more I researched and learned about CMU's engineering programs and their many links with technology companies across the country for career opportunities, the more convinced I became that CMU was the perfect academic fit for me. Not only is CMU among the top ten schools in ECE, it is also well known for its arts and humanities, it is only a two-hour drive from my hometown, and its financial aid package, which my parents and I estimated using the college's net price calculator, made tuition affordable. All of these factors combined led me to apply to CMU as an Early Decision applicant, a binding option if admitted. I was totally fine with this option because I was sure that it was my top-choice school and that it was financially affordable. Ultimately, the complete list of schools that I applied to included Case Western Reserve University, University of Michigan, and the Honors College at OSU, because all of them had non-restrictive Early Action options. Other colleges on my list that I would have applied to in the regular round, had I not been accepted into CMU, included University of Pennsylvania, Northwestern University, and Johns Hopkins University.

## What About Rankings?

*U.S. News & World Report, Niche, College Board, Fiske Guide,* and other online publications aggregate a lot of data in an effort to compare and rank colleges and universities in the U.S. While college rankings are heavily disputed, the information found in the college profiles can still be useful. Don't place too much weight on a school's specific ranking. In the end, what matters more is how well the school matches your dreams (and abilities).

I sat down with Nancy Beane, former president of the National Association for College Admissions Counselors (NACAC) and a veteran college counselor at Westminster Schools to get her perspective. "The best advice that I have, based on my 27 years as a college counselor, is to open your mind to the, literally, thousands of college options out there. It can be hard to look past the brand names; try to understand that there are so many good schools. Beane add, "You can get an excellent education and have a fantastic experience at one of the lesser-known schools. Conversely, not everyone thrives at what I call the whoop-de-do schools."

She cautions students to be careful judging a school by rankings and the things you see on the surface. If you really like (or don't like) the tour guide, for example, that may color your viewpoint, but try to look a little beyond that one personality.

*Most high school students, like myself, spend days and weeks looking at which schools have the highest rankings or have the lowest acceptance rates. I remember creating an Excel sheet that organized the schools I was interested in based on SAT score requirements, cost, and ranking. While it is indeed important to look at the academics of a school, it is also very important to research the environment in which you will be living for at least the next four years of your life. Visiting a school gives you an experience you can't get from reading Internet articles or browsing through brochures.*

—JASMINE AL-AIDY, GEORGIA TECH

## Consult with Counselors

Like Nancy Beane, the college counselors at your high school will have a valuable perspective of the college application process that is different from your own view or that of your friends, family, and the admissions representatives at schools. They often have a keen sense of how others at your school have fared at competitive schools and where students with similar academic profiles as yours have placed.

*If your school offers college counselors, take advantage of their knowledge, as they have likely seen hundreds or thousands of previous students find their way. While this varies by high school, my counselor turned out to be an excellent resource for many of my questions. In addition, she was able to help process a lot of the required forms/transcripts, reducing the amount of work I had to do. However, you will not always agree with your counselor's advice, and that's OK. Remember that ultimately, the decision of where to apply and attend is yours, and only yours.*

—ARIF HARIANAWALA, UNIVERSITY OF TEXAS AT AUSTIN

At some large public schools, the counseling department can be extremely busy trying to support a large graduating class. Be mindful of their time and try to set up a meeting if you would like their input.

> I talked a lot to my counselors and went to all college fairs the school hosted. My high school counselors were great at helping...but for one-on-one I'd recommend having a list of questions ready to ask your counselor and setting an appointment in advance to talk about career and educational options after high school.
>
> —Phoenix Rose Hoffman, Laguna College of Art and Design

Think of your counselors as just one of the important support systems in a multi-pronged approach to help you find your best-fit institution.

> I found it really helpful to go to my college and career center at school and talk to the guidance counselor there. It was scary at first, but she was very kind and helpful and she helped me explore my school options, provided me with tips for my applications and essays, and gave me more information about the college admissions process. Additionally, the Internet provides amazing resources. Almost every-thing is online nowadays, even all of your college applications! So I found that if I was ever confused about what documents I needed to submit, I would just go on that schools' admissions website, and all my questions would be answered. You can also find student forums and contact information for your schools that can provide you with some mini-networking in order to get even more information on various colleges and programs.
>
> —Shanaya Sidhu, UCLA

**College Fairs.** Take advantage of any college fairs that your school or nearby schools offer. It is a low-stress, inexpensive way to collect information and talk to admissions representatives from a wide range of schools. Browsing the tables and booths at fairs can also help you identify the types of schools that you do not want to consider.

Campus Visits. During your college planning process, schedule campus visits as early as possible. Nancy Beane says, "The best time to go on tours is your junior year. You will be too busy your senior year, especially if you are in sports or other activities where you are a leader or have commitments you must keep. Your coaches don't want you to miss games and practices because of school visits, and you don't need to let your team or program down by being away too much of the time. Teachers want you in class, and your primary responsibility is to be a student as a senior." More than anything, stepping foot on the grounds of colleges you think you want to attend can help you figure out which schools feel right and which ones don't. Visits can include an informational session, tour of the campus, and an interview with an admissions representative, if available. If you can't physically travel to a campus in person, spend time viewing virtual tours. Also try to stay in contact with the college admissions office and attend any local presentations or informal orientations.

*I went to CalArts for a tour during summer break and spent the whole day learning about the school and its current students as well as its alumni. It's really important to try and visit the schools you have an interest in and talk to everyone you can there. If you can't meet them in person, contact a counselor at the college you are interested in. Tell them your name and try to keep in touch because the more interest and commitment you show to a college the more they notice you. I had a virtual online tour led by a college counselor at Cogswell Polytechnical because I couldn't go visit them. My parents joined the virtual tour so the counselor could answer any financial questions they might have as well as educate them on the college itself. The talk and tour really helped me understand the school better, which made me realize that in the end, Cogswell wasn't the college for me.*

—PHOENIX ROSE HOFFMAN, LAGUNA COLLEGE OF ART AND DESIGN

Touring schools can help you drill down on some of the details that you might not be able to learn about until you are physically there. Student housing, dining halls, the feel of the library on a typical day—these are just a few of the things that are best experienced in person. Attending a short summer program at a university is also a good way to get a great sense of what the campus has to offer.

*I did tour the campus multiple times, both with the tour guide and on my own. I knew the campus really well already just from taking day trips up there to explore. I never did any college fairs but I did watch the virtual tours the colleges I applied to had available on their websites. I feel it is worth noting that it is important to also tour dorms. I researched extensively what dorm I wanted to live in. I knew what I wanted and what I didn't want. I didn't want communal bathrooms, I did want a roommate, I did want a laundry room on my floor. These factors helped me find the perfect dorm and roommate.*

—NATALIE CHANDLER, BAYLOR UNIVERSITY

Yet school visits can be expensive and logistically impractical. If you are unable to visit schools in person, there are other ways to get a feel for a school.

*There are resources in person, online, and over the phone that can help you make a decision without needing to travel. I did a Skype call with a Canadian university that reached out to my high school, and so I decided to apply there after learning more about them. Some universities offer live videos that you can join in on at certain times from anywhere in the world. Other universities have lots of photos and videos that can roughly equal a tour in person. Another good resource is also talking to people who have been there or attend that school, so reaching out to see who around you knows of the schools you are interested in, or even if they know someone that can be put in touch with you to answer all of your questions. Online reviews are often not very thoughtful, I've noticed, as people tend to focus narrowly on several experiences since a lot of reviews tend to be around a paragraph long.*

*Some universities are also open to being called for small inquiries as well as for detailed information. Interestingly, the university I chose to go to was one that decided to call me. I had been accepted, but I hadn't made a decision in about two weeks. I quite literally spent a full hour and a half on the phone with a representative from the school who answered all of my questions ranging from what living in Canada would be like and how I would find an apartment, to questions about programs and classes. After never visiting the university in person let alone visiting the city it's in, getting a call from someone enrolled there, who lives there, and was hired to know as much as possible about the school is what made me label it my first option.*

—JARON CHALIER, CARLETON UNIVERSITY, CANADA

## Fit and Feel

Nancy Beane points out how individual a person's response can be to a school when they visit. She says, "Students who go to similar high schools and have the same kind of education may visit the same school and have vastly different reactions to it. Sometimes your reaction to a school boils down to a feeling that you can't get until you step foot on campus." She recalls a story where she was surprised by the reactions of two of her students. "I once had two students visit a small liberal arts college in Vermont on the same day with the same tour guide and they walked away with polar opposite impressions. It was surprising because they were friends with similar interests and academic profiles. One liked the school so much that she pulled her early decision application from an Ivy League school to apply and ultimately go there. The other student said, 'I wouldn't go there if it were the last school on Earth.' They had the same weather, the same activities, the same everything. One loved it. The other hated it. It can be such an individual thing, like having a preference or dislike for a kind of food. That's why it's important to visit if you can. And if you can't visit, talk to friends you may have at the schools, take a virtual tour, try to connect with students and university representatives online or on the phone."

*When I started my college search, I had originally decided Texas A&M was where I wanted to go. It's where everyone in my town goes, where some friends and family go, and I have talked about it since elementary school. As I started the serious search, I realized it was not what I had in my head. I tried to imagine myself there and I couldn't. I knew it was not the right place for me since I didn't feel at home. I had been getting information and offers from Baylor since sophomore year but I never thought about actually going until I decided what I wanted to do with my life. Once I realized that, I knew Baylor was exactly what I wanted and needed. It was my dream school. There was no question about it. The moment I got that acceptance text, email, and saw the words on my laptop I knew it was where I was going.*

—NATALIE CHANDLER, BAYLOR UNIVERSITY

## Interviews

Some colleges will request interviews to get a better feel for applicants. You may also reach out to admissions officers for an interview. These can take place either at the campus or in a location close to your home by admissions representatives or local alumni. The best way to prepare for these interviews is to practice everyday conversation in a variety of settings and with a range of different people. "During each interview," says Lori Breighner, global recruitment officer at Duke Kunshan University, "you should be prepared to articulate why you are drawn to the school and to share your aligning interests and passions. Also, distinctiveness can go a long way—you shouldn't be afraid to showcase your unique personality and use humor (appropriately, of course)!"

The following college visit worksheet helped one student narrow in on his top choice school. Filling it out for each school can make it easier for you to compare features before applying. Feel free to modify this to accommodate your own specific criteria.

# College Visit Worksheet

*Complete the top <u>prior</u> to your visit.*

**College:**

Number of Students: _____

Location: _____

Date of Visit: _____

Three reasons I am interested in visiting this school:_____

_____

_____

Two majors that I find intriguing: _____

_____

Two clubs/extracurriculars I could join: _____

_____

Questions I have about the school:_____

_____

_____

_____

_____

How would I get here/travel time if I were to attend? _____

_____

**Facilities**

Campus Layout: _____

Classrooms: _____

Student Center/Hang out spots: _____

Library: _____

Dorms: _____

Dining Hall Meal Plan: _____

Restaurant/Grocery Options: _____

Athletic/Arts Centers: _____

Career Center: _____

Academic Buildings/Professors Offices: _____

**Students**

Overall Impression: _____

Enthusiasm for School: _____

Academic Intensity: _____

Diversity: _____

**Social Life**

Typical Weekend: _____

What are the popular activities on campus: _____

_____

What is there to do off campus? _____

Current issues on campus? (Pick up a newspaper!) _____

**Overall Impression**

Most Impressive Feature: _____

_____

_____

Least Impressive Feature: _____

_____

_____

My chance at admission: High, medium, or low? _____

**OVERALL ASSESSMENT OF HOW WELL THIS COLLEGE FITS YOU:**

Not very well    1    2    3    4    5    Extremely Well

Additional Notes: _____

_____

_____

_____

_____

_____

_____

_____

_____

_____

## Do Not Curb Your Enthusiasm

Every point of contact with a school can be an opportunity to show your interest. Whether through the college application essay, campus tours, interviews, or by directly connecting with admission representatives, you can proactively demonstrate your enthusiasm. Schools want to know when they are your top choice and can sometimes sense when you have another school in your heart.

This next student had such a clear goal of pursuing a military career that he thinks it may have hurt his chances with the Ivy League schools to which he applied.

CHRISTOPHER KIM,
U.S. NAVAL ACADEMY

In addition to school visits, I also attended Summer Leadership Programs at Harvard, West Point, and the Air Force Academy during sophomore and junior summers. I also attended Senior Fall Class Candidate Visiting Programs at Harvard, Yale, Brown, Coast Guard Academy, and the Naval Academy. Participation in these programs, demonstrated my strongest interest to these schools. I also interacted with each school admissions counselors as much as I was allowed to without breaking the courtesy. Through these visits, I learned that I have the best fit with Yale and all four Service Academies. These schools became my top priority schools.

By end of September 2017, the Naval Academy had given me a Letter of Assurance (LOA), guaranteeing admissions if I would change my Congressional Nomination to Naval Academy and get medically qualified by the Department of Defense Medical Review Board. I felt that even though my childhood aspiration was to become a Cadet at West Point, I was not going to give up a guaranteed Appointment to the Naval Academy. In October, I passed the medical review board. In December, I was given a Congressional Nomination by my Congressman. In January 2018, I was given a full Appointment by the U.S. Naval Academy. I had secured one of my top college choices.

During this time, I was appointed to the U.S. Coast Guard Academy by Early Action in November 2017. By February 2018, my safety school, Norwich University, offered me admissions to their 2022 class with full Provost Academic Scholarship in any major. With three offers, I felt very secure and I was elated to go to one of my top choice schools. On March 30, I was not offered a place at Harvard and was placed on the waitlist by Yale. By then, I knew that even if Yale and Harvard had given me offers to their class, I would still accept the U.S. Naval Academy Appointment in the end. I felt that the Naval Academy was my destiny. I loved everything about the Academy: the campus and the world-class facilities and professors; the academic program and choice of majors and minors; varsity athletic programs, leadership programs, and clubs; summer training programs abroad in foreign countries; sea trials, aviation, land, and submarine training; and internship at Cyber Intelligence Units at the NSA, Defense Intelligence, and National Cyber Operations Joint Command. I am also given career internship options at number of top defense and civilian companies such as Lockheed Martin and Boeing. And, of course, a guaranteed career in the Navy upon graduation. Plus, I am paid monthly salary of $1,200 to $1,400 that covers my student expenses with some spending money left over. Yes, free tuition, room & board, and free medical and dental, and discounted life insurance is offered. And finally, I will receive a full active duty military benefit while at the Naval Academy including shopping at defense department operated duty free shopping centers. This is absolutely hard to beat! The value of attending a Service Academy is $400,000 for four years. If the costs of training and military benefits are included, the value rises to $600,000.

What I learned from the admissions marathon this year, all top selective schools want to be your number one choice. Unless you are a sought after under-represented minority or someone with a very rare talent and gifted academics, these schools do not have to pursue you. They have thousands who are qualified to fill their class. I believe it was very clear to Yale and Harvard that I was not evaluating their schools as my number one choice given that my focus was attending a top academic program that can also offer top military training programs. I am certain this was evident from my activities, resume, and personal statements. Even though Yale and Harvard/MIT offer high quality ROTC military training programs, they are primarily intellectual communities that offer a part time reserved military training program to a highly select, small group of students who wish to commission as officers in the U.S. Military.

I believe I was an easy candidate of choice by all Service Academies. My profile, my history, and experience match their ideal candidate: Scholar, Leader, Athlete, and Volunteer. I also believe that all schools want to be your number one choice! If I had to do it all over again, I would probably choose one Service Academy and one top selective civilian college to be my number one choices. And make a clear presentation to each school. I felt that although my package was strong and persuasive, my essays and parts of my application to Yale and Harvard may have lacked my number one choice commitment to their schools, if given a chance to matriculate. Strong future candidates, make certain that schools you are applying to have no doubt that you are choosing their schools as your number one choice to make it easier for these schools to make you an offer.

# Refine

Your goal should be to narrow your college list to under 10 schools. Of course, your dream school should be on that list!

Consider applying to:

- 2-4 Likely (or Safety) Schools: you're confident you'll get in and you would be satisfied attending if no other options work out
- 2-4 Match (or Target) Schools: your statistics match with those required for this school and you have a defined interest in going there
- 2-4 Reach Schools: you aren't quite at the GPA or SAT levels generally expected by these schools, but you think you have some other factors that could potentially push you over the edge. Any Ivy League or any school with an acceptance rate of less than 10% is a reach unless you have won a Nobel Peace Prize or have been recruited for sports.

Nancy Beane says, "The ideal number of schools to apply to is six—two what we like to call foundational schools (ones where you feel certain you will get in), two realistic, and two reaches. You can apply to more than that, but I think more than 12 is crazy."

---

ARIF HARIANAWALA
UNIVERSITY OF TEXAS AT AUSTIN

One of my biggest regrets was applying to too many schools. This consumed a large part of my first semester during senior year, and looking back, there were a good number of schools I was accepted to that I would never have even considered attending. Here's my list:

**The University of Texas at Austin - McCombs School of Business**
**Northeastern University**
NYU Stern School of Business
UCLA
**Boston College**
Emory University Goizueta School of Business
Dartmouth University
UPenn Wharton School of Business
Cornell University
UC Berkeley
Duke University
**University of Oklahoma**
**University of Alabama**
**University of Pittsburgh**
**Reed College**
**Boston University Questrom School of Business**
**George Washington University**
**Indiana University - Bloomington Kelley School of Business**
**University of Maryland - College Park**
**Purdue University**
**Santa Clara University**
**UConn**
**The University of Illinois at Urbana–Champaign**
**The University of Rochester**
**UMass Amherst**

**University of St Andrews *UCAS (international application)**
Oxford University*UCAS
**The University of Edinburgh *UCAS**
**King's College London *UCAS**
**University College London *UCAS**

The schools I bolded are those I was accepted to, and those that aren't I was ultimately denied from post-waitlist or post-deferral. As you can see, there are a *lot* of schools here. Try not to apply to this many schools, as I can tell you from experience that it really isn't necessary or worth it.

As you can see from my college list, I applied to a number of Ivy League schools but wasn't accepted to any. While I started the college process hoping to be admitted to one, I ultimately realized that there are many, many others schools at which I would be just as happy and successful. Keep that in mind when applying, and it'll help you find the best option for you!

If you are keen on attending an Ivy League school, it is imperative that you do not view being accepted as a "make or break" situation. There are other good schools out there, and you will be fine if you don't get admitted. However, to best prepare yourself, it is important to strive for the best grades and test scores while making sure you are an involved and engaged member of both your local and academic community.

## Major Considerations

A common approach when looking for the best school is to evaluate different institutions based on how well their academic programs match up with your interests and intended major.

If you know your major or field, you can look at a school's strength and depth in that specific program.

*Once I identified my goals and values, I was able to make more proactive choices about where I wanted to apply for college. I have always wanted to enter medicine, so my choices were influenced by schools with good science and pre-medical programs. I started to think about where I wanted to apply for college towards the end of the summer before my senior year. I finalized my choices during September of senior year with the help of my college and career counselor and proceeded to apply. I actually did not have one particular dream school while applying. Since I did not have a set dream school, I applied to as many places as I could afford so that I would have many options to then decide what my dream school was. I felt a little lost at first, but with help from my parents and college and career center guidance counselor, I was introduced to more schools that may be a good fit for me. I benefit from a motivated learning environment and a great science program, so I applied to places such as UCLA, UC San Diego, UC Berkeley, USC, Claremont McKenna College, University of the Pacific's Accelerated Dental Program, Drexel University, and Arizona State University, among others. I also wanted to stay in California for the most part, so I applied to a lot of schools in state. It is important to consider both the social and academic environment of a school, since you are picking your new home for the next upward of four years.*

—Shanaya Sidhu, UCLA

If your parents are steering you toward one particular major or another, be respectful and open to listening to their ideas, but make sure you stay true to your inherent strengths and interests. "If you are interested in a liberal arts major and your parents think, 'Noooo you're not going to get a job!" try to reassure them," Says Nancy Beane. "That simply isn't true. Yes, it is important to put yourself in a position to get a job later, but plenty of employers seek out liberal arts majors with good communication and critical thinking skills. For your own peace of mind, visit the career center and look at the outcomes of the students in your intended major. What kinds of jobs are graduates getting? Where are they going to graduate school?"

*By deciding on a major, my college search was much easier. After narrowing down the schools, I was able to shorten the list even more by looking at the programs provided at the schools. I intend on majoring in communications and possibly minoring in business. With me wanting to major in communications, the school I once thought was my dream school turned out not to be a perfect match for me. The school I once thought was my dream school no longer met the requirements, making the search continue.*

—LANAE BARROW, BOWLING GREEN STATE UNIVERSITY

Yet Larry Schall, president at Oglethorpe University says, "I try to convince students not to pick a school based on its academic program because we see probably at least half of our students change their minds about their major." Another reason to keep an open mind about your major and your career, he says, is that "Research shows that students graduating in 2022 will hold more than 20 jobs and work for 12-20 companies. And most of the jobs that you will end up doing are not jobs that exist today." Being nimble and adaptable to change is important.

Not all schools require you to choose a major when you are applying, but many do. According to Nancy Beane, "You may be able to improve your chances of getting into a school by declaring a major that is less competitive at that school. You can ask the admissions representatives what their most competitive majors are or find that information on the school's website. If you can find one of the less competitive majors that is still relevant to your interests, you might be better off from an admissions standpoint." She adds, "Be careful, though, in assuming that you can transfer into a different major once you are there. Doing so may be possible, but sometimes it is not."

## It's OK to Be Undecided...at First.

There is an exchange between Alice and the Cheshire Cat in Chapter 6 of Lewis Carroll's *Alice's Adventures in Wonderland*:

> "Would you tell me, please, which way I ought to go from here?"
>
> "That depends a good deal on where you want to get to," said the Cat.
>
> "I don't much care where—" said Alice.
>
> "Then it doesn't matter which way you go," said the Cat.
>
> "—so long as I get SOMEWHERE," Alice added as an explanation.
>
> "Oh, you're sure to do that," said the Cat, "if you only walk long enough."

The lyrics from George Harrison's song "Any Road" echo this idea: "If you don't know where you're going, any road will take you there."

*I knew I would want to enter business since sophomore year, which made choosing a major easy for me. However, choosing a major, or even a field of study is not always this easy. Some tips I would recommend when it comes to doing so include looking at websites detailing professions that result from majors, and not being afraid of the undeclared option. Many students think that being undeclared hurts one's chances when the reality is that it doesn't. College is a time for exploration; if you don't know what your passion is just yet, use college to figure it out. It's better to take your time and find what you love than to be stuck doing something you hate as a profession.*

—ARIF HARIANAWALA, UNIVERSITY OF TEXAS AT AUSTIN

Feeling confused or uncertain about what you want to study or where you want to go is normal, and it's OK to be undecided at first. The following student's journey is a hopeful progression through the ambiguities and opportunities.

LAURYN DARDEN, NEW YORK UNIVERSITY (NYU)

Those four years in high school went by in a blink of an eye. Each year would pass, and I'd be amazed at how much time was going by. It was scary, but honestly, at the end of every year, I'd get more and more of an adrenaline rush. Those "what if's" would become more descriptive, practical, and more importantly, real. There was a sense of fear, excitement, and eagerness the closer graduation got. Though graduation was a finish line of a sort, it wasn't necessarily the end. Graduation only signified a new beginning. My curiosity would submerge each thought I had with one simple question —what's next?

Though you grow up, and many things change, people never want to stop knowing what you want to do with your life. A youth's future can exhilarate our older companions. As cliché as it may sound, kids are the future. Therefore, a lot of what we do matters to this world. Our paths and goals are ones that have been entreated, prayed, or dreamed about. Thus, when it comes to searching for what you are meant to do, and whom you are meant to be, do not get discouraged. During high school, it seemed like I wanted to be a million different things. One summer, I participated in New Haven's Law Camp and just knew I'd be a lawyer. I went to Yale and Eugene O'Neill Playwriting Retreat and just knew I'd be a playwright. I acted in three all-school theatre productions and just knew I'd be an actress. I even binged watched 13 seasons of *Grey's Anatomy* in two weeks and just knew I could be a doctor. Each of my ideal careers came from interests of mine. I'm very proud that I actively participated in many different things because it helped me figure out what I wanted to do with my life. Although, this did make figuring out which colleges to apply for very hard. I began to notice that all colleges are known for something different. Every school has certain rigorous programs, research facilities, renowned staff, and opportunities that will make you realize that the possibilities are endless.

When I first began going to college tours, it was mostly southern schools. I saw Clemson University, Howard University, Duke University, Spelman College, Jacksonville University, Furman University, Valdosta State University, and more. Every college I saw was amazing in its own way, but I needed to find what school would be best for me. Because I wasn't exactly sure about what I wanted to be towards the end of my junior year, I was overwhelmed. I thought that by then, I should have already known exactly what I wanted to be. I became worried because I had seen so many colleges at that point and still didn't know what I wanted my major to be. Or, where I wanted to go. Then I had my junior meeting with my guidance counselor, which gave me a new perspective on things. Through all the madness, stress, and the plethora of questions, I overlooked one simple and obvious thought. My guidance counselor told me, "You are young. Therefore, you have the luxury of being able to be confused and uncertain."

Hearing that, helped me realized that I didn't need to find the school that was best for my career. I needed to find a school that was going to help me figure out who I wanted to be. A school that would have enough resources for me to have a multitude of experiences. A school that would reveal my path if I couldn't yet see it myself.

Still confused, I took the summer to broaden my horizons even more. I was chosen to be part of a program called Center for Creative Youth (CCY). This program allowed me to reside at Wesleyan University for four weeks while having a major and minor. Because this was an arts program, I majored in Creative Writing and minored in Musical Theatre. I appreciated my time at CCY because it made me feel really comfortable being an artist. It was very inspiring because they advocated professional artistic careers while debunking the struggling artist myth. They brought in so many people who were successful with their art degrees. And for the first time, I was no longer confused. I knew that whatever passion I pursued, it had to be in the world of the arts. I returned home from CCY having a better idea of what I wanted to be surrounded by in a college, and in my future. A couple of weeks before school, I toured my first northeastern school—New York University.

Though I wasn't sure about much, I was certain I wanted to be far away from my home in Connecticut. But, when I visited NYU, I was blown away. While I was there, I could literally picture myself being a student. My favorite thing about NYU was the endless amount of opportunities. Whether it was an internship or a study abroad program, they understood the importance of experience. Also, I believed NYU replicated the real world. The world that can't be ignored. A diverse, multicultural world that each student and faculty member gets to really know how to be a part of. It was at that moment that I realized I didn't want to be the only, nor did I want to be a part of the only. Diversity became the first criteria on my college list. I knew that I wouldn't apply to many, or any, Historically Black Colleges/Universities. Nor, would I go to any school that was predominantly one race. NYU also made me realize that I needed a school that supported the arts and had a rigorous arts program. I was so happy that I visited this school because it became the first school on my list and my dream school.

One thing I learned during the NYU information session was that it was a 70 thousand dollar school, and their acceptance rate was below 40 percent. Though I loved the school, I felt really discouraged. Of course, I still applied, but I didn't feel confident about it at all. Because of this, I started to apply to schools that had bigger endowments. My guidance counselor once said, the bigger the endowment, the more money in scholarships the school is able to provide. Also, I decided to use College Board to create a list, which really helped. Their site ranks each school on your list as a safety or reach, based on your academic profile. My college list consisted of the following schools: Boston University, Howard University, New York University, Pace University, Spelman College, University of Connecticut, Wesleyan University, Western Connecticut State University, and Yale University. Each of these schools had art programs—specifically dramatic arts—that were innovative and supported. Also, all these schools were either diverse, had large endowments, small student-to-faculty ratios, or nice campuses.

Because I wanted to be in the dramatic arts like I had been in high school, whether it was producing, writing, or acting, some schools required auditions, portfolios, and interviews along with the college application. I auditioned for Pace, BU, and Howard. NYU was the only school that had a Dramatic Writing for TV, Stage, and Film major, so I sent in a portfolio of my writing there. The other schools didn't have these specific requirements for their drama departments.

These prerequisites made things even more stressful. There were more deadlines to keep up with and notifications to look out for. To help with that, I'd put each of those dates in either my calendar or remind app. Other than that, the college application process during senior year will have you questioning a lot. Personally, it raised a lot of insecurities for me. I was unsure if all my hard work in high school was good enough. I had breakdowns, I cried, I vented, and I didn't always believe in myself. For the first time, my future seemed so close to me, that it frightened me. My imagination was something that I no longer wanted to expand because it was becoming too scary. Those wandering, daring, optimistic possibilities that swarmed my mind for so long, weren't exciting me. Waiting for college acceptances was like holding my breath. My uncertainty about my future didn't intrigue me, it worried me. This is why I made sure that I worked hard on my college essay. I wanted my idea to be original and authentic. Because I was insecure about my academic life, I wanted my essay to show my character. With lots of revision suggestions from my teachers, that's exactly what it did. It told a story that exposed who I was, but more importantly, gave an insight into the person I am able to become.

Finally, Pace University mailed my acceptance letter, and I could breathe again. My first college acceptance letter restored hope in my self-esteem and future. I still told people I was applying for Yale and NYU for giggles, but some confidence for my future was still growing again. This was because Yale and NYU were the most prestigious colleges on my list, especially with Yale being an Ivy League. One thing I was adamant about was not applying to a school for its name. But, applying to a school because I genuinely believed the school could help me with my success as a scholar and growth as a person. Yale was the only Ivy League that had an undergraduate theatre arts program that I liked. NYU was the only school that specifically had a major for the type of writing I enjoyed. People shouldn't apply to schools just for their popularity. You have to make sure you love where you're being educated.

It was important to me that I loved each school on my list. That way, there would be no disappointment no matter where I ended up. I knew rejection was possible during this process. However, I also knew that I wouldn't end up anywhere I wasn't meant to be. Out of the nine schools I applied for, I got rejected from three —Howard, Wesleyan, and Yale. Truthfully, it bothered me for a little bit. But then, March 28 happened. On March 28 I found out I got into my dream school, New York University, with full tuition.

## Rethink and Rejoice!

Have you ever heard someone say that sometimes things happen for a reason? Do you ever feel as if fate or serendipity has been on your side? This story is for you. A seemingly sensible path for this student was rerouted with a gut feeling, an early decision application gone sour, and a happy ending!

ELISE E. SCHLECHT,
BARNARD COLLEGE

I remember the first time I started seriously thinking about applying to college. It was a fall night in 2012, and after finishing my homework I wandered into my older sister's room to spend some time with her. I found her poring over a book that detailed the college application process and listed all the top schools in the country. I asked her why she was doing all this research now, because at the time she was only a sophomore in high school. She looked at me and asked why I was not looking at these things already. "It is a really long process," she told me. So that night, we went over my options. I was happy; I was in eighth grade, and I already had a college list. It was a very inaccurate one, because, for example, I had the University of Pennsylvania listed as a safety school, but I had a college list.

Since that night, I always kept a list of schools jotted down somewhere; in the margins of a notebook, in a document on my computer, or in neon whiteboard marker written on a mirror on the back of my bedroom door for motivational purposes. I always had a list, no matter what I was interested in studying. I flirted with the idea of joining the Air Force, and going to Embry Riddle for aeronautics. I thought of going to Pratt for visual arts, being an anthropologist like Temperance Brennan, or just starting my own freshwater pearl farm. (This was a legitimate interest of mine for a while. I have no idea why my mother did not appreciate it.)

It took awhile for me to interpret my interests concretely, in the form of an academic subject. I have always had a passion for learning and knowledge, but I did not know where this could possibly lead. With the help of my favorite literature instructor, I explored my passions. I became his Teaching Assistant, a position I held for two years, during which time I wrote tests and quizzes and delivered lectures on Marxism, horticultural symbolism, and Russian short stories. Most significantly, however, he signed me up as a plenary speaker at a state-wide conference on Chinese mythology, an experience so profound that I would later write my admissions essay on the subject. On that day I found my calling—I was determined to become a professor, and I knew exactly what area of study I wanted to focus on for the rest of my academic career. Russian.

Since I was a child, I have dreamed of studying Russia, its language, history, and culture.

What started as a childhood fixation with ballet and its history in Russia, over time developed into a very real passion for the study of a beautiful and frequently misunderstood culture. I read as much Russian literature as I could get my hands on, researched the imperial history, and eventually wrote a thesis on the work of Vladimir Nabokov for my high school literature course.

Naturally, then, when I started looking at colleges, I gravitated toward those that had strong Russian programs. I knew I wanted a well-respected and historic school with good connections and a dedication to educating students to the highest of standards. I knew I wanted a small school, something that was not unlike my high school, where everyone knew everyone else and the learning environment was competitive, but not cutthroat. I loved the look of East Coast schools because they reminded me of my hometown, and even more importantly, the reputations of the schools were of the highest quality. However, I did not think that I would want to attend an Ivy League school because I thought that if there was going to be any sort of intellectual hierarchy at my college of choice, I would want to be at the top. I thought, and I know now that I thought incorrectly, that if I were in an Ivy League environment, I would fall to the bottom of the barrel and be disappointed with myself. So I set my sights on the smaller colleges and universities of note, specifically the Seven Sisters. Unfortunately, since Radcliffe was absorbed into Harvard, I only really had six sisters to choose from. I loved the idea of attending a women's college, of great female leaders being educated together in their own little cloister of knowledge. I liked Mount Holyoke initially, but deferred from applying. I liked Barnard, but it was in the city and it was connected to Columbia, which made me nervous that I would not succeed in comparison to my peers. Smith seemed too liberal, and Bryn Mawr was not picturesque, so I set my sights on Vassar and Wellesley. I loved Vassar, but the idea that it was coed was a slight deterrent for me, as I wanted the full women's college experience. So Wellesley became my school of choice.

I suppose it would have made much more sense for me to say that the school I had my heart set on was Barnard, but no. It was Wellesley. Wellesley College seemed to check every box on my list: a beautiful campus, spotless reputation, historic alumni, and most of all, a Russian Studies department founded by my own personal hero, Vladimir Nabokov. I was sold. So my mother and I went to Wellesley when I was a junior in high school. After all, junior year is the time for college visits! The campus was just as beautiful and the programs were just as glowing as ever, but I left with a vague sense of unease. It was nothing I could pinpoint at the time, but the experience had stimulated some anxiety in me that I could not bear, an anxiety that irrationally made me think that the best option for me was to stay home forever and never go to college.

That was the first and should have been the only sign I needed to know that I was on the wrong path, that Wellesley was wrong for me. But I was stubborn; I forced myself to fall in love with the idea of the school, and ended up convincing myself that I should apply early decision. And I did. And I immediately regretted it.

When I returned to the campus for my admissions interview, my mother could tell that something was wrong. I explained that I was concerned that my social life would not be what I wanted it to be, that I would like to be closer to the city and its excitement (as opposed to 30 minutes away by bus), and that maybe I might just miss having boys around a little bit. I was very torn up about my irreversible decision to apply E.D., and I had many a tearful conference with my school counselor on the subject.

So finally decision day arrived, and for whatever reason I was hopeful. Truthfully I think that maybe I was just a little impatient, and in retrospect I can see how I mistook that for hope. I pulled up my admissions portal, and read "We have decided to defer your application until..." and I burst out crying. I had just wanted the process to be over; just give me a firm yes or no, I do not want to be left hanging! The next day I was depressed, but it was softened by the fact that my close friends had also been deferred from their top schools. Not softened enough, though, because again I found myself crying in my school counselor's office.

I cried largely because I had done everything right. My essay, about discovering my call to professorship at the conference on Chinese mythology, was perfect. I had worked on it over a period of four months at least, with countless drafts, revisions, and edits, and by the time it was complete, it had been read by at least seven people who had given it their stamp of approval.

My ACT scores were well within the range required for admittance, but nonetheless I had been seeing an ACT tutor for months to give them a little extra push. My GPA was next to perfect. My letters of recommendation were written by teachers who had seen me grow and excel in their classes. I had college credits from accounting and advanced algebra classes, honors credit from chemistry and biology, and I had skipped a grade in literature and even designed my own curriculum for myself senior year when my school ran out of classes for me to take. I had AP English Literature, AP English Language, AP Art History, AP Human Geography, AP U.S. Government and Politics, and AP Macroeconomics on my transcript, with three 5s and one 4 already, and one score pending testing in May (the only course I did not take the test for was AP Macroeconomics). I had taken Spanish since first grade.

I was on the honor roll, an NHS member, an NSHSS member, a National Commended Student, and a State Senate Scholar. I was a member of the local youth orchestra, a state-ranked forensics competitor, a member of the Model U.N. team, an English T.A. and guest lecturer, a choir accompanist, a pit orchestra member, and the holder of a full-time job. I had individually completed over 250 volunteer hours knitting baby hats for a local hospital and helping elementary school teachers in Madison set up their classrooms. I felt that there was nothing I could have done to make my application more competitive than it already was. I had already pulled out all the stops, and there was nothing left for me to show Wellesley admissions that could possibly convince them of my merit if all this had not been enough.

On top of all this and offering no consolation whatsoever was the fact that at the time I had only received admittance from one other school, which I was definitely not going to attend. It was the University of South Dakota, my super safety, to which I had only applied because I would receive the in-state tuition rate as the child of an alum. They did not even have a Russian Studies department.

My counselor said to me that all I could do now was look at other schools until Wellesley made their final decision. So I made another list. And literally two hours later I was sitting in her office again, saying, "I really should have applied to Barnard earlier." I had read a little about Barnard the summer before senior year, having picked up a copy of *The Hidden Ivies*, and I was intrigued. It had the top-notch academics I was looking for, the community of high achieving women, and the recognition of an Ivy League university behind it. At the time, I had been afraid of the big city. But not anymore.

Barnard became my new dream school, and I knew that I had been foolish not to apply to the college sooner. I had read about it in the summer, and it had seemed incredible. But I had been scared, and I was scared simply because I thought the city would be too big for me and that Columbia would be too big a pond to swim in. But after my reservations about Wellesley and my desire to be closer to civilization, and to boys, I decided to look more into the school that almost could have gotten away. I immediately fell in love. Barnard was exactly what I was looking for: it was small, beautiful, and shared a Russian Studies department with Columbia, a department overseen by the Harriman Institute, the nation's premier institution for the study of Russia, Russian culture, and the history of the Soviet Union. The community was close and inclusive, and it was right next door to some of the greatest museums, parks, and cultural experiences that the world has to offer. The campus, as seen via Google Earth, was as picturesque as I had imagined my dream school to be. I was sold, even more so than I had been with Wellesley, and I decided that this would be my new home, if they would have me.

My application to Barnard was unlike any other application that I had sent in. For one, I submitted it over a month before the required deadline. Although I always respected application deadlines and started my applications well in advance, I was never confident in submitting applications very early because I feared that I might overlook some crucial detail. I wanted my essays to be perfect, my lists of extracurriculars to be perfect; everything had to be perfect, and I had to feel it. I felt this perfection with my Barnard application. I had applied to Middlebury, Williams, William & Mary, NYU, Colgate, Colby, and Vassar, but none of my applications were written with as much excitement and energy as my application to Barnard. I was enthralled by their essay topics—I was eager to discuss which woman from history or fiction I would have coffee with, and detail a time when I "majored in unafraid." I was even excited to explain why I felt that Barnard would be a good fit for me. These supplemental questions were unique in that they provided a look into the personality of the college and the mindset of those who excel there. I was convinced that Barnard and I would be a perfect fit.

I anxiously waited to hear back from Barnard. While I had applied to nine other schools, Wellesley and the University of South Dakota included, I hardly cared what my admissions decisions were. Colgate and Colby were the first to say yes; I was happy to receive a positive response, but I hoped that there was a better one coming. Middlebury, Williams, and NYU came back with waitlist offers, which were not entirely disappointing, and William & Mary and Vassar both sent back an enthusiastic yes. Wellesley came back and said they did not want me, but at that point, I felt that I did not want them. I mean, would you go to prom with a guy who said, "I will take you, but only if no one hotter wants to go with me"?

The day I was admitted to Barnard, I was sitting in the quiet study room of the public library, unsuccessfully trying to focus on my Human Geography homework. I opened my admissions portal at 5:00 p.m. sharp, and saw that beautiful, beautiful word—congratulations! I jumped out of my chair, did a happy dance that I am sure looked ridiculous to the other patrons of the library, and ran out into the low-voices-allowed area, where I called my mother and whispered the happy news. She was so proud of me.

The first time I set foot on Barnard's campus was eight days before the enrollment confirmation deadline, when my mother and I came to the city for admitted students' weekend. Despite the fact that we both knew that Barnard would be the place for me, I was nervous. To be honest, though, that was something that I had come to expect from college visits. The decision to uproot your life and transplant it in another city or state is a big one, and no matter how exciting the prospect, because the prospect of college is incredibly exciting, it is a decision that is bound to stimulate some anxiety.

So I was uncomfortable as we filed into the Ella Weed Room to hear a presentation by the admissions staff. The first thing they did, though, allayed all my fears. They began to read excerpts from our letters of recommendation. As they read, I tried to identify among the excerpts one that could have been written by my literature teacher and mentor. I was amazed, because all of them could have been. I saw a piece of myself in each of the girls they described, and it gave me the confidence I needed to know that I was in the right place.

My name is Elise E. Schlecht, and I am a sophomore at Barnard College, the women's liberal arts college of Columbia University in the City of New York. I am double-majoring in Russian Language & Cultural Studies and Art History with a visual arts concentration. I am a volunteer SAT tutor, the Social Chair of the Columbia Quiz Bowl Team, a sister of Alpha Omicron Pi, a nationally ranked Russian-language essayist, and I could not be happier with my life at this moment.

# The Application

Here we are folks! Lined up at the starting gate for the big race. All of your years of preparation and hard work has brought you this far. Now you have to prove yourself to a group of complete strangers for the privilege of four more years of hard work and preparation. Oh, and for the pure delight and camaraderie of the college experience. It's all worth the effort. Hang in there for this next phase, because it can be a challenge.

Think outside the box in terms of how you present yourself. College admissions counselors often see thousands of student applications, so it's important to be creative and highlight yourself in a way that helps you stand out as a unique student who's genuinely interested in being a part of their university.

Also be aware that many colleges are paying more attention to applicants' emotional intelligence and kindness quotient in addition to academics and achievements. They are looking for evidence of empathy and respect for others. The Dartmouth College Tuck School of Business recently announced that it was looking for candidates who exemplify four qualities: smart, nice, accomplished, and aware. One of its new essay questions for MBA applicants asks students to share an example of how they helped someone else succeed. People submitting recommendations are asked to comment on how the student interacts with others including when the interaction is difficult or challenging. They are looking for authentic examples and endorsements that reveal a student's character. A former Dartmouth admissions officer tells a story of a surprising letter of recommendation from a school janitor that illuminated the student's unprompted and consistent kindness and consideration to everyone at the school, no matter what their position. That application went straight to the accept pile!

A 2016 report called "Turning the Tide: Inspiring Concern for Others and the Common Good through College Admissions" created by "Making Caring Common," a project by the Harvard Graduate School of Education and endorsed by 80 colleges admissions professionals and other stakeholders, emphasized that both ethical engagement—especially concern for others and the common good—and intellectual engagement are highly important in the college admissions process.

# Getting Organized

*I think I only managed it as well as I did thanks to my meticulous planning in accordance to deadlines through a mobile checklist and Google calendar.*

—ABBIGAL MAENG, AUSTIN COLLEGE

Managing your time and staying on top of deadlines is easier said than done, but it can help produce incredible results. Here are a few of the major dates to keep in mind:

- August 1 - the Common App Opens (Make an account!)
- October 15 - a Major Deadline for those applying to international schools (Oxford + Cambridge Deadline)
- November 1 - The General Early Action / Early Decision Deadline
- December 1 - Scholarship Deadlines for many schools
- January 1 - Regular Decision Deadline for many schools
- May 1 - National College Decision Day

*When time inched closer to applications becoming available, I made sure to look at each school's site frequently and write down deadlines and important dates. I like to keep a planner and hand write things down since I remember them better that way. A phone is a good way to keep track of dates too but I prefer the old-fashioned way. I had sticky notes full of dates, times, lists of what I needed, who to talk to if any issues arose, passwords, usernames, and about a million other things written down. I kept all that information in a folder and then I kept all my online information in a folder on my desktop. I found that applying first thing and getting the required documents turned in and submitted as soon as I had them was the best method. Getting the application completed means it is reviewed sooner and an acceptance comes sooner. That was my way of thinking to get me motivated to get everything down as soon as possible. The entire process can be very overwhelming and seem like a lot but like with anything, carving out time every day or even a full weekend to do applications keeps the deadlines and dates in check and prevents any rushing or unnecessary/avoidable stress.*

—Natalie Chandler, Baylor University

It doesn't matter what system you use to stay organized and on top of deadlines as long as you pick a method—whether it's paper or digital—and stick to it.

*Prioritization was key in helping me stay on top of due dates and deadlines for all of the colleges I considered, because I would often be working on several applications at one time, especially with scholarships. Even though I wished I could complete everything at once, I forced myself to make a note of which applications were due the soonest, and then work from there. I made myself ample "to-do" lists and post-its with reminders to keep me organized and focused on one task, paper, or form at a time, and I tried not to succumb to the stress that accompanies tackling numerous projects at once. When I did start to let the stress get to me, I tried to release it in a positive way, such as using it for motivation to type just one more paragraph or fill-in one last application, because I knew that finishing part of my workload would help ease some of my anxiety.*

—KATHLEEN CICERO, EASTERN MICHIGAN

Even the most organized students can feel stressed and overwhelmed. When that happens, try to break things down into smaller bits that you can tackle one step at a time.

*I will be honest with you: this was one of the most stressful processes in my life so far. I am already an organized person, but I had to get even more organized. I set reminders on my phone, marked off dates on my print and digital calendars, created folders in my email account, kept my papers organized, and kept a digital note of things I needed to do with deadlines. I would check my digital note almost every day, setting a to do list for every day so that I would not miss a thing.*

—EYRAM AKAKPO, UNIVERSITY OF AKRON

In addition to college application deadlines and the due dates for your regular school work, you will need to keep the financial aid and scholarship application dates in mind. The FAFSA application for federal financial aid is open from October to June, but each state and each college has its own specific deadlines. Many private institutions also require the CSS Profile, which is available from The College Board.

SHANAYA SIDHU,
UNIVERSITY OF CALIFORNIA, LOS ANGELES (UCLA)

The process of applying was stressful because of all of the different deadlines. There are deadlines for college admissions applications, scholarships, financial aid applications, etc. You have to complete your FAFSA and CSS profiles for financial aid by a certain time, send in your test scores by a certain time, submit your transcripts by a deadline, and complete your application by a hard deadline. And even for the application itself, there were different deadlines! You could apply Early Decision, Early Action, or Regular Decision (and sometimes there were two different early decision deadlines or a merit scholarship deadline). So as you can tell, there are **tons** of deadlines to keep track of. The best way to get organized and avoid stress is to create some sort of spreadsheet. I created one on Google sheets. This spreadsheet was a lifesaver because it displayed all of the various deadlines for my schools and the forms I needed to submit for each school in one place. The columns on my spreadsheet included the school's application fee, application deadline (including whether or not they had some special deadline I wanted to apply by such as Early Action, which is non-binding, or a scholarship deadline), type of application (University of California application, Common Application, or if the school had its own online application), required amount of letters of recommendation, required number of essays, deadline for submitting test scores, and other important application information if applicable. That way, I could efficiently mark up my calendar with deadlines and get more organized.

## Spreadsheet Column Suggestions

- Application Fee
- Application Deadlines
  - Early Decision (binding)
  - Early Action (non-binding)
  - Regular Decision
  - Deadline for Merit Scholarship Consideration
- Application Type
  - Common App
  - Coalition App
  - Universal College App
  - State Specific (University of California and State University of NY, for example)
  - School Specific
  - Supplemental
- # of Letters of Recommendation
- # of Essays
- Financial Aid Deadlines
- Scholarship Deadlines
- Transcript Due Dates
- SAT/ACT Submission Dates
- AP Scores Accepted
- Admission Decision Dates

# Common App, Coalition App, and Universal College App

The good news is that many colleges and universities now accept standardized applications that you can fill out and submit to multiple schools with the push of a button. This can simplify the application process and save you a lot of time. The bad news is that there are several of these templated applications and different schools accept different ones. Deciding which among the Common Application, Coalition Application, and Universal College Application you should complete will depend on the colleges that are on your list. Also be aware that some schools still have their own specific application. And most will ask for supplemental materials in addition to the information in the application form.

"When applying to college, choose your application format wisely," says Nicholas Lim, Assistant Director of Admissions, Seton Hall University. "Many students make the mistake of starting the Common Application for an institution, but they will then start the institution's application. This causes issues when it comes to processing their transcripts and test scores. I always suggest to my students that they use the Common Application, if possible, if they are applying to three or more schools to make their lives easier."

## Special Cases

While it's true that some colleges may have entire applications or sections of them that are school-specific, you may also have special considerations that will need to be explained. There are ways to do that, even on the standardized applications. The University of California colleges, for example, recommend that you provide school context. If you attend a school that has an alternative curriculum, schedule, or approach to learning, consider working with your school to create a brief paragraph (within the Academic History section in the UC admission application). Understanding of the context for each student is critical. Contextual information includes academic and non-academic resources and opportunities available, what you chose to do or what you could not do and why. Being able to better understand the school setting can help the reviewer better understand you.

# Standardized Tests

Many schools publish data summarizing the profiles of admitted students from previous years, which can give you an idea if your SAT/ACT scores are in the ballpark. *The CollegeBoard's BigFuture* website is a fantastic resource for identifying if your standardized test scores, GPA, and courses put you on track with any given school.

The landscape appears to be shifting as more and more schools drop the standardized test requirement from their applications. The University of Chicago was the first highly selective school to drop its SAT/ACT requirement beginning with the 2018-19 application. Other universities may follow that lead because they won't want to lose potential applicants who have decided not to share their SAT scores (or who have decided not to take the tests in the first place). For the near future, however, the tests are still very much a part of the application package and you will want to give them your best shot.

Most if not all four-year schools will take either the SAT or the ACT. According to the ACT, more students have taken the ACT than the SAT in the past seven years. More than two million 2016 high school graduates took the ACT. Some scholarships may be set up specifically for one set of scores versus another, so it may be in your best interest to take both. Fee waivers are available. ACT issued $36 million in fee waivers during the 2015-2016 academic year.

*Taking the SAT/ACT, as well as submitting your scores to multiple schools can be expensive! Ask your school counselor for College Board fee waivers to register for exams and submit your scores for free! Applying to college can be costly too, with application fees up to $90. However, most colleges will offer fee waivers for students who need them, so confirm with your high school counselor that you quali-fy, and then reach out to the college's financial aid office for fee waiver codes to submit in your application.*

—Maile Harris, Yale University

Be sure to check each school's specific requirements. And plan to take tests early. In California, for example, the UC system requires the SAT with essay or ACT with writing be completed by the December test date of the senior year prior to gradua-tion. You must report a planned test date on the admission application, which must be submitted by November 30. Students who attend schools where the language of instruction is NOT English are also required to take English proficiency exams.

*My biggest piece of advice actually pertains to testing for applications: the SAT and ACT. I took the ACT four times and worked so hard in preparing and working on test strategies. Take the test as many times as you can or need to. Higher scores mean higher chance of being accepted and possibly more scholarship aid.*

—NATALIE CHANDLER, BAYLOR UNIVERSITY

Though you can go into the test cold, with little or no preparation, most people agree that studying for the tests and taking practice tests will help you improve your scores. In general, the more you prepare for these standardized tests, the better you are likely to do. There are tips and strategies for taking the tests that can help your scores. You can improve your scores by taking free practice tests (visit PrincetonReview.com/events, ACT Academy, and Khan Academy) and by taking the tests more than once. Here is a first-hand example of a student whose diligent preparation yielded superb results.

TEJNA DASARI,
UNIVERSITY OF TEXAS AT AUSTIN

I took the SAT, ACT, and the subject SAT's in Physics, Chemistry, Math I, Math II, and U.S. History. Time management and test scheduling were a crucial part of my being able to take all of these tests. I took my first and only SAT prep class the winter break of my sophomore year of high school and I took my first SAT the October of my junior year. I took a course in Houston from a company called TestMasters and I personally thought they were very helpful in terms of having an extremely useful curriculum, strategies, and instructors. One thing TestMasters had that I was glad to take advantage of was a program called Exam Club. This program allowed us to come in at any proctoring time (schedule would be on their website) and take a full-length test of any kind. So the summer before my junior year, I spent Friday and Saturday nights at group tutorial sessions for extra strategies and word problem workshops. I took a full-length test on

Tuesday, Thursday, Saturday, and Sunday mornings. I would review my incorrect questions the day after and see what I could fix. Other resources I used to study were definitely Khan Academy's SAT resources and practice tests. They were the best material anywhere. I used the following books for strategies and practice questions: *Cracking the SAT Premium Edition* by Princeton Review, *Math Workout for the SAT, 4th edition* by Princeton Review, and *Reading and Writing Workout for the SAT 4th edition* by the Princeton Review. I thought all of these books had really great drills. I liked the way the Princeton Review had drills and strategies and their books were straight to the point and very helpful to learn from. I got 1460 the first time, 1490 the second time, and a 1430 the third time, but they super scored into 1510, which crossed my goal of 1500. I used Princeton Review books for subject SATs as well. The ACT, I took on a whim and did not do too much practice except for one practice test a week the summer after my junior year. I did use the official tests on their website, which were extremely useful and I did use this one book: *The Real ACT, 3rd Edition*. The book is a little bit outdated and the ACT tests have gotten harder since, but it is a very good starting point and is very accurate in terms of types of questions to know and subjects to study. I loved this book. I scored a 34, on my first try.

Remember, test scores are only ONE of many parts to your application, so try to keep that in perspective. Staying relaxed can also help your scores! But even perfect scores are no guarantee. Schools will reject students with perfect 1600 SAT scores in favor of an applicant with some other quality that will add balance and interest to its community.

# Letters of Recommendation

Think carefully about who you would like to write your letters of recommendation. You want someone who knows you well and can write a compelling, anecdotal description of you that will bring out your best qualities. These letters can provide evidence of your intellectual curiosity, positive character traits, skills, and achievements. In addition to letters from educators and counselors, recommendations from supervisors, coaches, or someone who knows you well can also be helpful if they provide additional insight.

> *I believe this is a very important component that is often overlooked. I am sure a lot of people could get a good recommendation letter, a letter that praises how good of a person they are. But I believe the most important aspect of this letter is its individuality. It is very important that the letter fits you personally, the less cookie cutter it is, the better. The content of this letter should just be like the essays, where if your name is deleted, it could not be replaced by others. So in order to get a personalized essay, you should let your school counselor/teacher know you personally. I am very lucky that I come from a relatively small school where the teacher and student relationship bond is strong. Sometimes, I would email teachers about random personal thoughts I have, asking for advice. Talks with teachers do not have to be limited to academics; sometimes they do offer beneficial life advice. Hence through such interactions, my teachers were able to know me more on a personal level, allowing them to write up a better-fit letter for me.*

—ALISON SIN, CORNELL UNIVERSITY

Be considerate of people's time when asking for their recommendations. Ask them well in advance of your deadline and then follow up two weeks before they are due to make sure they still have time.

> *I got four letters of recommendation, two from high school art teachers and two from Palomar art teachers. Notify the people you want letters from as early as you can and remind them if needed later on. Make sure they can do it because if their schedule is tight and you're in a crunch you might need to find alternatives.*

—PHOENIX ROSE HOFFMAN, LAGUNA COLLEGE OF ART AND DESIGN

## How to ask for Recommendation Letters

DO

- Find an educator with whom you can discuss your extracurricular activities, college aspirations, other classes, etc.
- Provide your recommender with all of the information they will need to prepare and submit your recommendation.
- If you are required to provide a recommender's email address so that he or she receives an official recommender request, make sure you have entered it correctly!
- Read the application requirements carefully—an application may have a limit of one recommendation, may allow more than one, or may require more than one.
- Make sure to give your educator friendly reminders weeks before your scholarship deadline.
- Give thanks! Surprise them with a hand-written thank you card (not an email or social media post!).
- Maintain communication.

DON'T

- Ask for a recommendation at the last minute.
- List someone as a recommender or reference without their knowledge.
- Skimp on the information they need to prepare and submit the recommendation.
- Take it personally if the educator is not able to prepare a recommendation for you.
- Use a relative or family member for a letter of recommendation.

Russell Davis, who is the director of Global Student Recruitment at Duke Kunshan University, says "Applicants should help their recommenders convey those things that are most important to them. Ideally, recommenders should know the applicant so well that they can provide insight into what kind of student they are and how the applicant impacts the classroom. They should also be able to help the applicant tell their story. Prior to submitting their recommendations, applicants should meet with their recommenders and let them know what those activities, involvements and/or achievements are they plan to highlight in their application. In that way, the recommenders can provide another perspective on those involvements, and perhaps even give insight into how the student has had an impact *outside* the classroom–in the student community and even the broader community–as a result of the student's interests and passions. This reinforces the themes the applicant has chosen to highlight in their application."

## Demonstrating Your Passions

Another way you can demonstrate your important involvements and passions is "to connect your interests to the clubs, activities and programs at the university to which you are applying," says Russell Davis of Duke Kunshan University. "For example, if you enjoy photography and have highlighted an involvement in a student publication in high school, look for those university student publications where you can continue that interest and incorporate them into their essays when possible. This serves two purposes. One, it demonstrates the deep interest in that activity; and two, it allows you to show your strong interest in the university by showcasing the level of research you have done into the school."

# The Essay

Follow the prompts, tell your story, be authentic, and shine!

A well-written application essay that offers insight into your personality, values, and goals can go a long way in helping you stand out during the admissions process. Your college application essay should be both highly personal and thoughtful. Not only should your essay reflect well-constructed writing, but it is your opportunity to tell your unique story. Be creative and present yourself in such a way that embodies the real you.

*When it comes time to apply, start writing your essays early and of-ten. Create your application accounts the summer before your senior year so you have access to the prompts as soon as they are released. The more time you have to think about and craft your essays, the better they will be. Remember, colleges don't want to see a perfect candidate from your essays; they want to see your personality, what makes you unique and memorable. After you click "submit" on your application, it is assigned to an admissions counselor at the college who reads your file and is responsible for making your case to the admissions committee. The essays are your chance to showcase the challenges you've overcome, your passions, and your personality. They should show what makes you tick, and what makes you memorable. For example, I wrote about how my love of Star Trek drives my love of physics (and my fluency in Klingon!), and how I've met my mortal enemy in automatic sliding glass doors because I tend to walk right into the glass. I would argue that your essays are the most important part of your application, because although your grades and test scores may say "you're qualified to be here," the personality that comes out of your essays is what tells admissions officers "you deserve to be here."*

—MAILE HARRIS, YALE UNIVERSITY

Most students will end up writing several essays.

*In addition to your common application essay, many schools will ask you to write shorter "supplemental" essays to help them get to know you better. These are a good chance for you to showcase your knowledge of the school you are applying to and your fit for those schools. The best advice when it comes to these essays is to* **follow the prompt***. Many students end up writing about something other than what the school asked for, leaving a bad impression of the appli-cation as a whole.*

—ARIF HARIANAWALA, UNIVERSITY OF TEXAS AT AUSTIN

Supplemental questions can range from the quirky (Create your own spell, charm, jinx, or other means for magical mayhem) to the quintessential (What is the best invention of all time?). Another common supplemental essay prompt asks applicants to describe why they want to go to a particular school. See the "Why NYU?" example below. Be sure that your answers to any of the prompts reveals something about you—how you think, what matters to you, and what makes you different.

### 2017-18 NYU COLLEGE ESSAY PROMPT/RESPONSE

### WHY NYU? (400 WORD MAXIMUM)

### NICHOLAS WRIGHT, NEW YORK UNIVERSITY (EARLY ACCEPTANCE)

The summer of 2017 was a pivotal point in my life. My aspirations to deepen my understanding of international relations and to strengthen my leadership skills were realized when I was accepted as a summer intern at the United Nations. My interest in global issues began in 7th grade in as a member of the Kentucky United Nations Assembly club. I was fascinated with learning about other cultures and looked forward to our annual conferences where groups were assigned specific countries to study then problem solve in the social, politics, education, and economic challenges of that country. I was offered the opportunity to sit in the room with world leaders each day and learn what is involved in the hard work it takes to make positive change in our world.

To study International Relations at NYU's School of Arts and Sciences would be the most pragmatic step I can take for my future. NYU is endowed with multiculturalism, and that cohesion is what I find so attractive. NYU's academic community is a microcosm of New York's multi-ethnic melting pot. While there are many colleges like this, none come to the same level of organic diversity. That is the environment I foresee myself thriving in and making the impact I know I can make.

I experienced so much personal growth during my time in NYC during my summer internship. As a young person it's sometimes easy to doubt where you fit in the world and just how you can affect positive change. During my time inside the UN, I researched the correlation between poverty and education in third world countries and how certain economic relationships with more developed countries perpetuate the disparity. I prepared a presentation that supported my findings and proposed solutions. This work was very fulfilling not to mention the amount of knowledge I gained and shared.

I have been a member of the Muhammad Ali Center Council of Students since my freshman year of high school. I have a longing to continue the work I am involved with at the Ali Center. NYU is where I have to be. I see my future realized within the walls of your institution.

Consider making slight modifications to one essay to make it work for another school's prompts. But be careful not to just cut and paste in a way that will seem obvious.

*Now, you may have heard that essays are the most stressful part of applying to colleges. In my opinion, keeping up with deadlines was the most stressful part, but that may also be because I was not entirely sure of all the places that I wanted to apply to in the beginning of senior year. However, some essays were more stressful than others. Sometimes the prompts are fun; for example, one of Stanford's prompts asked you to reflect on an idea that makes you truly excited to learn. On the other hand, though, it was more stressful to write essays where you had to boast about yourself or discuss how you would contribute to a school. However, it also came in handy that I could use some of my essays from one school to address the prompts at other schools. This is really helpful when you have a lot of essays, and many of the prompts are asking similar or the same things. It's always okay to reuse college essays for other colleges, and it is often very efficient in saving time and energy. I also made sure to make a strict plan for writing the essays. Each week, I would write all of the essays for two of my schools. They did not have to be perfect, just drafts. I would write whatever came to mind, and then organize the information and edit it later. Then, I shared all of these essays with people I really trusted, like family, my best friend, my English teacher, and my college and career counselor. Their suggestions truly helped perfect my essays. The key, though, is to start as early as possible and not procrastinate.*

—SHANAYA SIDHU, UCLA

## Select a Compelling Topic

According to Brad Schiller at PROMPT, a service that helps students with the essay writing process, "Students tend to write about the wrong things. We've seen countless essays about music, drama, athletics, family, a single community service experience—I can go on. While all of these topics can be made compelling, most efforts leave the reader with a poor understanding of the student."

Schiller says there are two types of content that make for compelling personal statements:

- A Time of Personal Growth—Great essays commonly show a clear change by describing how you were before a specific experience (or set of experiences) and how you changed as a result of the experience(s). A time of personal growth can be any experience where you can discuss a clear change in yourself, such as overcoming a challenge or obstacle, finding your view of yourself or others changing, or finding your skills improving rapidly as a result of your own actions.

- A Passion—Great essays paint a picture of what gets a student excited. Most students have something that they just do or learn about for fun. It's typically something they are much better at, care more about, or spend more time on than the vast majority of their peers. For example, just being in band isn't enough—a lot of people do it. Rather, it can be compelling to write about spending a significant amount of time outside of rehearsal honing skills that led to becoming one of the best musicians in the band.

Here's a student who took the Journey approach in her Common App essay and the Passion approach in her supplemental essay.

ALISON SIN,
CORNELL

Given that I was never a journal kind of girl, suddenly having to delve deep into myself imposed a huge challenge. Who am I? What are my passions? This is the section I believe made me a more competitive applicant. I wrote my Common Application essay on my biggest insecurity. Through recounting experiences of overcoming my insecurity in different events, I saw myself through a different lens. I saw a girl who never relented, who pressed on and continued to place herself in situations where she would constantly be on the verge of anxiety. She is a courageous girl who has gotten stronger after each experience, and that girl is me. I started to appreciate myself more. I saw more good in myself. Without all the essays that I was required to write, I would still be that lost sheep who doesn't know herself, her values, passions, weaknesses, insecurities, and lastly, strength. Self deprecation is the modern trend influenced by the media around us, constantly pointing out our flaws and amplifying our insecurities. We start to forget about how good we each are.... We are each unique and are destined to bring different things to the world. Through this period of self-exploration, I saw myself grow to be a less judgmental and more compassionate person, toward myself and others. I started enjoying more of the little things in life, and developing more gratitude and happiness. And by reflecting such in my essay, I believe it helped me get into Cornell.

In my supplementary essay, I wrote about psychology as my passion. Psychology unveils the covers of our tightly sealed brain, allowing me to find plausible reasons for my thoughts or feelings. Intrigued by how each individual is driven to behave a unique certain way or to develop certain thoughts, I want to know what makes us who we really are on the inside. This interest naturally leads me to psychology. And this is what I wrote in my essay. Although psychology was never a subject offered at my school, I decided to transform my 'hobby' into a self-study academic interest by reading extensively about the subject and taking university courses in different universities in Hong Kong. And this is how I proved my passion to administration officers."

**Be authentic.** Don't write what you think the admissions team wants to hear. If you're not authentic and you're writing something you think somebody else wants, that's a formula for disaster. Admissions representatives say that the majority of essays look the same. Students who stand out should have essays that stand out as well.

Natalie Chandler,
Baylor University

At the end of the day though, who you present yourself to be to the admissions board is what matters most. Be yourself and honest. Don't pretend to be what you think the board wants in a student or what you think the "ideal" student is. Colleges want individuality and unique, diverse students. Use things about you to your advantage. I am a first-generation college student so I used that to my advantage. Many factors do play in the application process. If a traumatic or definitive event happened, write about it. Appeal to the admissions boards' emotions. Often events that are difficult impact who you are as a person and really end up molding you. Show the board how it molded you. In my essay, I used this as a strategy. My mother died when I was young, I had some serious health complications and have anything but an easy life but all the bad things brought to where I am now. I am in such an unbelievably positive and happy place in my life where things couldn't be any better. Who I am has been molded by these events because they had serious impact and changed my life thus changing me. I have learned lessons from them and grown stronger and grown into a better person from them.

It's OK to write about failure. Many students think that it is detrimental to mention failure, but when positioned correctly it can show tremendous strength. If you can show how you dealt with failure and the steps you took to learn and grow from the experience, it can reveal a strong level of maturity and thoughtfulness.

Be confident. Believe in yourself, take care of your business, get your work done, and don't let things overwhelm you.

*Be you, and be confident in yourself. Thousands of other students have the same GPA, SAT scores, community service hours, and extracurriculars, but you are unique from them because of your morals, experiences, and beliefs. Highlight these. This is what colleges will remember. If you have the option to write an essay or not, do it. It is your one time to express yourself, and it is critical that colleges see that you are a human being and not just a GPA-driven machine. You have many aspects of your life so let colleges see that. Show them that you are well rounded and involved in activities that define who you are.*

—Autumn Satterfield, North Carolina State University

## More Essay Writing Tips

- **Follow Directions:** Abide by the essay's guidelines. If an essay has a maximum of 500 words, writing 1,000 words will not give you an edge over other applicants.
- **Stick To The Topic:** Don't try to force an essay you have previously used into a topic that doesn't fit.
- **Be Specific:** Include plenty of details; don't generalize.
- **Quality Over Quantity:** If you plan to write about your extracurricular experiences, it is better to have thrown yourself into all opportunities afforded to members in 1-2 clubs or organizations than to have merely been listed as a member in 3-4 clubs or organizations.
- **Read Aloud:** Reading your essay aloud helps you determine how your essay will read to its reviewers.

- **Seek 2nd And 3rd Opinions:** Share your essay with your parent or guardian. Then, run it by a friend or a mentor for a more objective opinion without familial bias. Emily Pacheco, Outreach and Admissions Specialist, International Programs, UC Berkeley Extension, adds, "Ask for help. No student should think that they can write an essay on their own. You want multiple people's input. Also, just because you get good grades on your English papers doesn't mean you are a good writer. College essay writing is a different kind of writing."

# BE CREATIVE and Be YOU!

Don't bore the admissions committee. Imagine if you were reviewing hundreds of essays; what would make YOUR essay stand out from the rest? Feel free to use quotes, historical and current event references, or even pop culture references. Nancy Beane, Associate Director of College Counseling at the Westminster Schools says, "Make sure your essay is lively—that it jumps off the page—not long and boring!" She adds, "Tell a story you can be enthusiastic about. One student came to his college counselor with an essay that was kind of boring. She asked him about one of the volunteer roles that he had listed, and his eyes lit up. He told her about this elderly neighbor who asked him for help finding her newspaper one day. They struck up a conversation and that turned into a regular job where he helped her with her groceries and other chores through the years. She urged him to write about THAT rather than the long catalog of biographical information. He ended up writing a terrific essay that began, 'Young man, can you help me find my paper?'"

KAYLA CAMPBELL,
OHIO STATE UNIVERSITY

It took me a while to select a topic that completely resonated with me. I attempted a variety of the prompts in order to get a feel for them and ultimately the topic regarding *"an experience that led to growth through learning about myself and others"* completely caused my pen to fly. The topic truly resonated with me at the time due to my growing passion about our global community because I previously had the opportunity to travel abroad. I spent about two months on my main college essay because I like to take time to reflect and receive feedback. With those two months, I reviewed and revised my essay at least once a week. Sometimes I had to remind myself of the importance to let ideas settle in order to avoid a daily revision. During each revision, I spent no more than two hours before letting it rest. This was also crucial because I did not want to overwhelm myself by mismanaging my time for the essay process as well as my other involvements, especially school. My high school had a writing center that I worked with very closely. I would email my document to the professionals and then would sit down with them a few days later to discuss different aspects of my essay. I began my supplemental essays after I felt more comfortable with my main essay, which was about a month after multiple revisions. With those, I sent them to our writing center where once more they provided me with support and feedback. Overall, I kept up with deadlines by writing them into my planner. I wanted to apply early action and as a result I put due dates into my planner multiple times, giving myself a weeks' grace for each hard deadline.

# Worksheet for Giving Feedback on Personal Statements

**(Courtesy of PROMPT)**

**Instructions:** Have anyone who reads your essay fill out this four-question worksheet. It will help you improve the content and structure of your essay.

1.  **What did you learn about the student?**
    Write 1-3 sentences on what you walked away understanding about the student. Focus on how you would describe the student (e.g., values, personality traits)

2.  **Is the content compelling?**
    Does the content provide a clear sense of what makes the student unique, what the student values, and what sets the student apart from their peers?

3.  **What didn't you learn that you wanted to learn?**
    These are the questions that pop into your mind but go unanswered such as...

    *   Who were you before this experience?

    *   What did you learn from this experience? (i.e., how did it change you?)

    *   What have you done recently that is a direct result of this experience?

    *   How does this experience tie with your future ambitions?

4.  **Is the essay well structured? How can it be improved?**
    *   Do you think "accept" from the beginning to the end of the essay?

    *   Do you have a sense of where the essay is heading at each point in the essay? (i.e., there aren't parts that leave you thinking "How this is relevant?")

    *   Does the introduction "hook" you into wanting to learn more?

    *   What content can be cut and where can more content be added?

    *   Consider providing a short, example outline of how it could be restructured

Here is one student's creative and original approach...

TEJNA DASARI
UNIVERSITY OF TEXAS AT AUSTIN

I stepped off an old-fashioned railroad train that would no longer be of use; although, it would be fondly remembered as a mode of transport to an ancient magic school. I stepped onto a cobblestone street of London as I stared at the cars circling the clouds at the top of the Big Ben, people flashing in and out of thin air in the snap of a finger from one end of Trafalgar Square to the other, and the occasional broomstick soaring above or beneath the London Bridge leaving a streak of lightning in its trace. Letting out a deep breath, I glanced into the future. A future where "magic" exists almost solely through science. A future where platform number 9 ¾ at King's Cross Station in London is a remnant of times long past.

It is a society where people don't disappear in and out of air because of magic, but a society where people disappear in and out of air because of modern day technology. A future where everyone has the ability to de-materialize and re-materialize themselves in another location through a process known as beaming. Using photon particle scanners, it would be possible to replicate your body's atoms and then store the data in bits and binary code and send it through the Internet's infrastructure and DNS server systems to the IP address of your desired destination. However, the prevailing problem today is that to store those 1,000 trillion trillion atoms that the human body is estimated to be composed of requires storage that is 2 trillion times the size of the entire Internet system and would take more time than conceivable.

It is a society where flying midair using broomsticks is not accessed with the aid of charms, but a society where flying midair using broomsticks is made available with the use of modern day mechanics and software. Using motor powered brooms, ordinary people, not just those of magical lineage, would be able to accelerate through the air. They use this broomstick as a way of transportation and as a professional sport. These motor-powered brooms would employ jet propulsion to take off, use mechanically-generated air pressure to maneuver vertically and use the tail of the broomstick as a turning fan to navigate horizontally. This is in stark contrast to the pitiable yet admirable efforts of today's college students running around the ground with brooms between their legs, imagining that they are soaring through air, while embarrassed onlookers watch from afar.

It is a society where people don't vanish from sight by a cloak enchanted with invisibility, but a society where a person can vanish from sight by manipulating light and photons through a specially engineered cloth. These engineered materials are composed of metals and plastics that are arranged in repeating patterns that are smaller than the wavelengths of the electromagnetic material they are affecting. Here, they have the ability to bend light photons in a way to warp around the object, rendering them invisible to the naked eye. A future where a person can quite literally melt into their surroundings. However, we currently lack the technology for these materials to be mass produced in a cost-efficient way.

The fate of these future inventions that could have the ability to transport the matter of the human body or bend the nature of light photons to our will is left in the hands of today's quantum physicists and software developers. Modern day technological innovations and research are growing at a rate faster than ever, accelerating us to a world where the line between technology and magic is becoming invisible. That is the world I desire to be a part of. That is the world where technology prevails and magic is no longer needed. At the moment, my fingers are itching to help create this "magical" world through science and technology.

## Fairy Tales Can Come True (It Can Happen to You!)

Brad Schiller of PROMPT says that successful essays give the reader "a sense of the student's values or personality traits, and what the student hopes to accomplish in the future." This next student channeled her inner Mulan to reveal important aspects of her identity and how they relate to her plans for the future.

ESTHER BEDOYAN
CARNEGIE MELLON UNIVERSITY

My junior year English teacher always used to say, **"When someone asks you what your college essay is about, the correct answer is always 'me'."** Keeping this valuable advice in mind during the college essay brainstorming process, I first thought of important traits or personal experiences that I wanted colleges to know about, then established the proper vehicle to convey the message. I thought about what made up my background and identity, because the main objective of the Common Application essay is to enable colleges to become familiar with you as a person, as most academic and extracurricular accomplishments can be gleaned from other aspects of a student's application. I was one of only a few girls in my more advanced Science, Technology, Engineering, Math, and Medicine (STEMM) classes, and I always felt an overall lack of female representation in the engineering fields. My personal experiences with gender inequality in STEMM and at school not only made me work harder in high school to prove that girls are as equally skilled in STEMM as boys are, but it also motivated me, in part, to choose engineering as my career path. Because gender equality in STEMM, and society, is important to me, I wanted this aspect of my identity to show through on my college applications. I also wanted to emphasize other personality traits to colleges, such as my growth in self-confidence as well as drive and determination, because these traits are dimensions of myself that cannot be seen from test scores and grades. To tie all of these pieces together, I naturally chose the vehicle of the Disney movie Mulan. I had not only grown up admiring and loving this film, but I also saw myself represented through the movie and saw myself as a modern Mulan. When completing the Common Application essay section, I first wrote the essay without really considering what prompt to write off of, because there is an option of an open prompt on the Common Application, where the applicant can write an essay of their choosing. Then, once my essay was finished, I decided to categorize it under this prompt:

Prompt: Some students have a background, identity, interest, or talent that is so meaningful they believe their application would be incomplete without it. If this sounds like you, then please share your story.

I felt this prompt was most fitting, because throughout my essay I discuss how being a woman in STEMM has shaped my identity as well as my college and career choices.

*"(Be a man)*

*We must be swift as a coursing river*

*(Be a man)*

*With all the force of a great typhoon*

*(Be a man)*

*With all the strength of a raging fire*

*Mysterious as the dark side of the moon"*

In the 1998 Disney movie, *Mulan*, our heroine's one opportunity to impress the all-important matchmaker ends catastrophically. Not only does Mulan set the matchmaker's buttocks on fire ("scandalous!"), she is also too skinny to bear sons ("disappointing!"), and, worst of all, she speaks without permission ("unacceptable!"). As an Asian-Caucasian girl who grew up admiring this woman warrior, I see that modernized versions of the gender expectations Mulan battles on a TV screen still exist today—and it is my job to combat them.

When I volunteered at a local hospital the summer before my junior year, I experienced something akin to a punch in the gut. A caregiver who had stopped to chat asked my male partner, "Do you plan on being a doctor?" He said yes. She then smiled at me. "And do you plan on being a nurse, honey?" I politely responded, "No, I am considering being a doctor too, or an engineer." Though I knew of the pervasive gender gap in STEMM fields, I had never before encountered such blatant gender stereotyping. "Scandalous! Disappointing! Unacceptable!" However, I was determined to be the Mulan of the Imperial Army; I would be not only as good as, but better than my male counterparts.

I did not have to wait long for an opportunity. Five of 18 students in my AP Physics 1 class were girls, and only three of 15 in my AP Calculus BC class were girls. In both of these courses, I became accustomed to the low-voiced whispers accompanied by loud guffaws regularly emanating from an all-boys table. At first I was self-conscious, paranoid that the whispers following each question I asked were an affront to my inquisitiveness and intelligence. However, once I realized that my willingness to ask questions enabled me to master class material as well as, if not better than, my male peers, I no longer cared about the insignificant details of those murmurs. My confidence stemmed from my mindset that I had trained through hard work, not from the perceived opinions of others.

This confidence was tested as I, the youngest student in my grade and the only girl in my event, became Extemporaneous Speaking captain last year. At first, tasks I assigned would not always be completed, and certain teammates would tease me for asking them to contribute more. However, I aspired to help my teammates become their best selves, so I continued encouraging them to work harder. As their speeches improved and I won their respect, I understood that obsessing over their initial opinions would have barred me from building a successful team. This year, as Vice-President of Speech, I am one of only two girls on the Speech and Debate leadership team of 11 students, and only a quarter of the entire team is female. Instead of being intimidated by the inner circle of boys, I aim to make our team culture welcoming to girls, encouraging them to exit their comfort zone and forget about the pressure to be cautiously perfect, as I ultimately did.

Instead of being "quiet and demure," as was expected for Chinese brides, Mulan is proud, powerful, and unafraid in a military for men only. As I make my way in a male-dominated engineering field, I continue to embody Mulan and "woman-up." I hope to be compassionate yet courageous, polite yet powerful, fashionable yet fierce. I may not be perfect, but I will be brave.

*"(Be a **girl**)*

*We must be swift as a coursing river*

*(Be a **girl**)*

*With all the force of a great typhoon*

*(Be a **girl**)*

*With all the strength of a raging fire*

*Mysterious as the dark side of the moon"*

# 2018-2019 Common Application Essay

Arif Harianawala,
University of Texas at Austin

The Essay. This task is one that many students either worry about excessively or put off until the deadline. Both are tactics that are only going to harm you. When it comes to the essay, the best advice I can give you is to start early and get as much feedback as possible. Ask your teachers, friends, parents, and even coaches to review your essay and point out what you may have missed. This will make you more confident in your writing and convey your effort to the admissions officers.

The Common Application offers seven prompts that can help spark your imagination. This list was taken from the Common Application website and will remain the same for the 2018-19 application cycle.

1.  Some students have a background, identity, interest, or talent that is so meaningful they believe their application would be incomplete without it. If this sounds like you, then please share your story.

2.  The lessons we take from obstacles we encounter can be fundamental to later success. Recount a time when you faced a challenge, setback, or failure. How did it affect you, and what did you learn from the experience?

3.  Reflect on a time when you questioned or challenged a belief or idea. What prompted your thinking? What was the outcome?

4.  Describe a problem you've solved or a problem you'd like to solve. It can be an intellectual challenge, a research query, an ethical dilemma—anything that is of personal importance, no matter the scale. Explain its significance to you and what steps you took or could be taken to identify a solution.

5.  Discuss an accomplishment, event, or realization that sparked a period of personal growth and a new understanding of yourself or others.

6.  Describe a topic, idea, or concept you find so engaging that it makes you lose all track of time. Why does it captivate you? What or who do you turn to when you want to learn more?

7.  Share an essay on any topic of your choice. It can be one you've already written, one that responds to a different prompt, or one of your own design.

The most popular essay prompt of the 2017-2018 application year (through January 5, 2018) is "Discuss an accomplishment, event, or realization that sparked a period of personal growth..." (23.6%), followed by the topic of your choice option (22.5%), and "Some students have a background, identity, interest, or talent that is so meaningful..." (21.4%). The last prompt, which is essentially a "choose your own topic" was introduced relatively recently and introduces new levels of flexibility for you. The best way to choose a topic is to think of something that is of meaning to you, and that you feel defines you in some way. This can range from writing about cereal to writing about an experience you had.

For me, the essay process was a long one. I began drafting my essay at the end of junior year, and although my topic stayed the same, my actual essay changed dramatically up until a week or two before the early action deadline (November 1st). I chose to write about a program I have been a part of since 6th grade, and how it has changed and shaped me as a person. Kids4Peace was instrumental in shaping me as a person and helping me grow into a unique person, which is why writing about it was an obvious choice for me.

Here's my Common Application essay:

I am a terrible singer. In elementary school, I would weasel my way out of chorus nights or take cover behind the classmate in front of me. Yet here I was, smack dab in the middle of a group of high-strung, enthusiastic, and overbearingly loud campfire song singers.

This was the summer after sixth grade, and I was one of 24 kids selected to be part of Kids4Peace Boston's first summer program. Half of us were from Jerusalem, having either Palestinian or Israeli backgrounds, and the rest were from across New England. We hailed from three different religions: Christianity, Judaism, and Islam. As the singing finally died down, one of the counselors asked: "How was your first day?"

I looked up, shielding my eyes as a cool breeze blew smoke from the crackling fire into my face. At that moment, I wanted nothing more than to describe how much I loathed being at this experimental camp, and how much I resented being forced to attend. Unfortunately for my sixth-grade self, my parents were insistent that I give this camp a chance. Reluctantly, I swallowed my frustration and kept my mouth shut as my peers conveyed their excitement for the weeks to come.

I woke up the next day, steeling myself for another day of inane conversation and cacophonous songs. After breakfast, I met my "peace buddy," who was from Jerusalem. The topic of discussion assigned to us was the Israeli-Palestinian conflict. "Here we go again," I thought, preparing to make an awkward attempt at maintaining a conversation. Instead, I sat in shock as he described various near-death experiences and how he had become accustomed to losing friends and family to the conflict. As I listened, I felt shame building up inside me. My complaints about the camp seemed inconsequential and ignorant. For these kids, the camp was an opportunity to experience what it feels like to not have to constantly worry about being bombed or beaten.

The Israeli-Palestinian conflict is a sensitive topic, and discussing it evoked a lot of emotions. Tensions ran high. Disagreements erupted. Despite not having a bias towards either side, I got a glimpse of what it would feel like to live amidst such tension every day. I tried to act as a mediator of sorts when disputes got too heated. Slowly, we made progress, learning to stop and think before responding to each other. By the end of the camp, while tensions still existed, we had learned to listen to and be accepting of each other's perspectives. And we still sang songs. As my new friends sang heartily, I raised my voice, off-key and all, and joined it with theirs.

Fast forward to July of 2016 as I packed my bags, reminiscing on the years since that first time I attended the Kids4Peace camp. Despite the time I had spent learning more about the Israeli-Palestinian conflict, practicing de-escalating arguments, and thinking critically about possible ways to lead the two sides to a peaceful resolution, I was nervous. This time I was going as a counselor-in-training. Would I be successful in teaching this new batch of to-be "peace leaders" the values of Kids4Peace?

As I led the group through their first campfire songs, I mentally picked out the kids that were starting camp with reservations, as I once did. I wanted to pull them aside and reassure them, tell them how this experience would inspire them to understand and accept others' perspectives. But I refrained. I knew that they would have to come to this realization by themselves. It would take place over a period of weeks, months and years of introspection and reflection.

My experiences with Kids4Peace over the last six years have not changed the fact that I am a horrendous singer, but they have inspired me to turn my voice into a symbol of hope for those who need it.

This essay is by no means perfect, but it's what worked for me, and if you spend enough time editing and revising your essay you can easily meet or exceed this standard! Also, while this essay did include references to politically divisive issues, I stayed away from taking sides and instead focused on my experience and self-growth.

## 2017-2019 Coalition App Essay Prompts (500-550 words)

1.   Tell a story from your life, describing an experience that either demonstrates your character or helped to shape it.
2.   Describe a time when you made a meaningful contribution to others in which the greater good was your focus. Discuss the challenges and rewards of making your contribution.
3.   Has there been a time when you've had a long-cherished or accepted belief challenged? How did you respond? How did the challenge affect your beliefs?
4.   What is the hardest part of being a teenager now? What's the best part? What advice would you give a younger sibling or friend (assuming they would listen to you)?
5.   Submit an essay on a topic of your choice.

## University of California Essay Prompts

The University of California application has its own set of eight essay prompts and asks applicants to select and respond to any four. Representatives at the University of California recommend that you choose the Personal Insight Questions that best reflect your individuality. Consider how you would respond to all eight questions before making your final four selections. Responses are valued equally; the "best" questions are the ones that allow you to present yourself authentically.

Even if you are not applying to UC schools and the prompts on your dream school's application may be different, it will serve you well to think about these questions and how you would answer them. These are the kinds of questions you may be asked in admissions interviews, job interviews, and over dinner or coffee with potential friends. The prompts challenge you to think carefully about yourself, your values, and what makes you tick.

1.   Describe an example of your leadership experience in which you have positively influenced others, helped resolve disputes, or contributed to group efforts over time.

2. Every person has a creative side, and it can be expressed in many ways: problem solving, original and innovative thinking, and artistically, to name a few. Describe how you express your creative side.

3. What would you say is your greatest talent or skill? How have you developed and demonstrated that talent over time?

4. Describe how you have taken advantage of a significant educational opportunity or worked to overcome an educational barrier you have faced.

5. Describe the most significant challenge you have faced and the steps you have taken to overcome this challenge. How has this challenge affected your academic achievement?

6. Think about an academic subject that inspires you. Describe how you have furthered this interest inside and/or outside of the classroom.

7. What have you done to make your school or your community a better place?

8. Beyond what has already been shared in your application, what do you believe makes you stand out as a strong candidate for admissions to the University of California?

Here are the four University of California essays that helped Shanaya Sidhu get into UCLA:

SHANAYA SIDHU
UNIVERSITY OF CALIFORNIA, LOS ANGELES (UCLA)

For the University of California campuses, the application fee was $70 per campus. I spent roughly a month writing, editing, and perfecting these essays for the UC campuses. There were eight prompts to choose from, and I chose four that would showcase my dedication and passion towards other people and pursuits that I care about, which was the underlying theme of my four essays.

**Ripples of Change** (Question 1)

The days passed by at my job as an instructor at Kumon, and I always noticed him. He was still struggling. Other instructors either told him he should know how to do the problem, hurriedly explained it once, or just got frustrated and ignored him. I could see and feel his pain of being intellectually belittled, and I was determined to not let him have this sort of learning experience at such a young age.

Andrew was an eight-year-old student enrolled in the math curriculum at Kumon. Everyone considered him a problem student, since he was easily distracted, but I knew that was not the case. People either get distracted from their obligations when they do not want to apply brainpower or do not know how to do so, and I knew Andrew's case was the latter.

One day, as Andrew passed by my table, I stopped him and told him to sit with me. Typically students sit across from the instructor, but I waived this custom temporarily so that Andrew could finally receive the attention he needed. Throughout the lesson, I encouraged Andrew and rewarded him with smiles and high-fives, even when he failed. He slowly began to improve and eventually even moved up a level in math. Having Andrew as a student taught me that positive reinforcement is one of the most important aspects of leadership. No matter how my day was going, I drew up courage and radiated a smile for my students, and they, especially Andrew, always appreciated it. For me, leading a group is about dedicating myself to others and not letting my own troubles consume me or negatively influence the way I treat them. I've learned to lead by example while focusing on each individual and using positivity to push them to their full potentials. Each individual has the power to impact themselves. This causes ripples of change as others begin to follow the example set by that individual, even if the example is simply confronting leadership and life with unwavering positivity.

**Mere Ink Marks on a Page** (Question 2)

I remember my first time. I was 15-years old. The sun beamed through my window, blinding me as I stared at my wall. Summer was passing by as a hot, boring buzz. I was involved in different art forms, such as drawing and singing, but I hadn't yet found one that truly spoke to me as an individual. Creativity must stir a passion within people that pushes them to pursue and master a certain art form. I wanted to be more creative, but I hadn't found my muse yet.

My eyes rolled across the room, searching for something, *anything*, to do. My fingers grazed a black ink pen on my desk, and I began to lightly drum with it. I then came across a slender, brown journal on my dresser. Grudgingly, I brought the journal back to my desk.

There were so many possibilities.

A blank paper staring back at me.

A pen grasped in my hand.

I began to write a poem about my grandmother. The pen seemed to glide across the paper and elegantly sketch words before my mind could catch up. I felt a sort of adrenaline rush as I dug the pen tip into the white surface. I began to write daily, and poetry slowly became my muse. At first, I was hesitant to share my poetry with others, but I realized that art is something to share and discuss, so I began to show my poems to my family members, and I even recently submitted some poems to the Poetry Foundation for publication.

Poetry allows me to drain my grievances and emotions and make meaningful ink marks with them. Ink marks that speak. Ink marks that add to my inner fire. Ink marks that empower me and give me confidence. The fact that scratches against a paper can convey emotions, intelligent thoughts, and, most importantly, creativity inspires me to continue writing and confidently expressing myself both on paper and verbally.

**Physiological Wonders** (Question 6)

Reaching out, tweezers in hand, I grasped for the toy butterfly within the man's stomach. I was so close. Almost there. *Buzz!* My ears filled with the electric vibration indicating the extraction was a failure. Although it was just a game, growing up, Operation was a small way of living my dream.

Science, specifically anatomy, is my biggest fascination and has made me seem pretty strange at times. In preschool, when asked about what it was that I wanted to be when I grew up, I answered with surgeon rather than the typical answers of superheroes or butterflies. In middle school, while most people cringed at the black, slimy liquid oozing out of the cow eyes during dissections, I watched in awe at the sneak peak into a biological function to which I had a front row seat. Even now, while most people think a scab is disgusting or irritating, I view it as a physical manifestation of the wonderful healing powers of the human body, which is composed of mere atoms just like everything else on this planet.

My love for anatomy drove me to spend my summer before senior year shadowing Dr. Taylor at Los Robles Hospital, where I had the opportunity to not only temporarily quench my thirst for science, but also solidify the lifelong speculations I had of the medical field.

Over the summer, I witnessed surgeons, a.k.a. hospital celebrities, performing heart surgery with fancy telescope gizmos attached to their heads while casually chatting about Wimbledon. Intensivists, like Dr. Taylor, intubated patients and placed central lines as if they were reciting the alphabet. Everything seemed so normal to them, and that is, oddly, what inspired me the most.

To be able to one day feel that saving people's lives and making a huge impact on the world is *normal* seems like such a far-off goal. However, no matter how long entering the medical field takes, I know my insatiable hunger for science and anatomy will drive me to pursue and accomplish my goals.

**Mastering Foreign Forms** (Question 3)

My hand was gripped around the racket as if I were holding a hammer. The movements felt so unfamiliar and awkward. I had never played tennis before, but the sport enticed me, being that it was a strategic game and lifelong pursuit. At tryouts, I wasn't extremely bad, but I wasn't extremely good either. I was just mediocre, and that did not satisfy me.

2014-2015: Junior Varsity #1 Doubles.

I contacted my Junior Varsity coach and asked if I could have extra lessons. I would sometimes come at six in the morning and practice until the afternoon on weekends. Slowly, my strokes became a bit more natural. It still was not good enough. I would sometimes have a five-hour lesson and then rush to team practice. My muscles burned, but it was only a sign that I was working as hard as I wanted to.

2015-2016: Varsity #3 Singles.

All the hard work paid off, and I was ecstatic to play on the Varsity team. Sadly, though, singles just wasn't for me. I had always played team sports, and I needed someone to work with.

2016-2017: Varsity #1 Doubles.

I continued having lessons with my Junior Varsity coach to push my limits even though I already achieved my goal. I received the Most Improved Award two years in a row, and my doubles partner and I had a record-breaking winning streak with only one loss the entire season. We even got to see our names on our coaches' hall of fame plaque for doubles, our local newspaper, and the Ventura County "First Team," which includes the county's best high school tennis players.

My improvement in tennis has shown me once again that if I truly strive for a goal, I can obtain it through hard work. Knowing that my life is within my control, I want to continually strive for the best and make every opportunity count. By this philosophy, tennis has become my greatest talent, and, in the process, reinforced my strong persistence in overcoming any obstacles in my life.

## Essay Structures

Essays need to control what the reader is thinking at each point of the essay while also keeping the reader engaged," says Brad Schiller. "Start strong by 'hooking' the reader and providing a clear sense of where the essay may be heading. In addition, essays need to cover not just a single moment or experience in a student's life but also provide context for who the student is before that moment and who the student now is today as a result of that experience. We find there are two effective structures for personal statements—'the journey' structure which is more of a narrative and 'your passion' structure which is more of a montage of many events and experiences."

DOMINIQUE DEMPSEY,
AMERICAN UNIVERSITY

*"I am too dark."* I said to my kindergarten teacher as tears fell uncontrollably from my eyes.

I did not understand what I had done wrong. My classmates and I were playing with jumbo cardboard blocks when we got the idea to combine them and build a giant fort. After working together and completing the fort, I tried to enter but was stopped. "Why can't I come in Cindy?" I asked my classmate, puzzled. "You can't come in because you are too dark."

I wish I could say that I stood up to her, but I did not. Instead I ran and I hid beneath a playroom table in the corner and sat "crisscross applesauce," watching broken-heartedly, as my classmates played.

In retrospect, I can now say at the age of seventeen, that I understand how experiencing racism at a young age can change the trajectory of a person's life. My painful experience as a five-year-old created an indelible imprint on my life. Kindergarten was the last time I ran from a conflict without seeking a solution.

It caused me to seek out and find my voice. I discovered an open forum where I could develop my voice of advocacy and joined the Debate Team. Ethics bowls, speech meets, and debate tournaments allowed me to develop critical thinking skills that would yield my strong desire to present well developed arguments for a cause. It also became a place where I could passionately offer researched-based information for change.

Conflict, struggle, and challenges are painful but they are also great incubators for growth and success. My experience as a child has become catalytic in developing my voice as an advocate for people who have experienced unfair treatment and or injustices based on religion, race, gender, or skin color. I aspire to obtain a degree in international relations. I also yearn to incorporate my passion for the arts with programs and policies that will positively impact people around the world. I will utilize my degree and heart passions to comfort the hurting, to confront the issues, to consider and create solutions, and to educate others. My story has become a message of hope.

## Channel Your Inner Superhero

This student felt that by explaining his interest in superheroes, he could convey his passions.

EDUARDO GONZALEZ,
UNIVERSITY OF CHICAGO

I hardly remember my first time seeing the first Spider-Man movie. I just remember that I absolutely loved it and that I wanted to be just like Peter Parker when I grew up. Consequently, as I grew up, I made sure to consume all superhero media and products made available to me. As I look back at my childhood, I quickly realize how superheroes were always there for me, slowly molding who I was. Once, my mother bought me a Spider-Man book, but this was no ordinary Spider-Man book; I was a character in it and I helped save the day. I reread that book countless times. My brain never stopped to think that the book was not written especially for me by Stan Lee himself. It did not matter, it made me feel special and I cherished it until I, being the careless little kid that I was, lost it only to be found by my adolescent self years later. While that book's stay with me may have been short-lived, its impact was not. "I can be a superhero. I can make a difference," I constantly thought to myself in those early years. Those thoughts disappeared into my subconscious as I embarked into elementary school, but I never stopped loving superheroes.

Once I was in sixth grade, my classroom was assigned a project to map out our entire life: past, present, and future. We had to answer every-thing from how many pets we had all the way to what we were going to name our kids. As I read through the questions, there was one that seemed to be glaring at me and it quickly caught my attention: "¿Qué vas a hacer cuando seas grande?" What was I going to do when I grew up? My first thought was that I had to dedicate myself to something in the area of science, my best subject along with mathematics. As kids we don't know very much about the opportunities that life has to offer us as adults. We seemed to be limited to the options of teacher, doctor, lawyer, and whatever our parents dedicated themselves to. My second thought was that I wanted to do something to help people. That little strain of superhero in me was working its magic on me without my noticing. After concluding that being a science teacher was not going to be helping anyone, I settled for doctor. "But what kind?" I asked myself. After little to no thought, I decided to write I wanted to be a veterinarian since that seemed to be the most popular answer among my peers. I reiterated that answer to anyone who would ask for the next few years of my life even though I knew that was not what I wanted.

It was not until quite a few years later that I had the definitive answer. I had known it all along: I want to be a superhero. This does not mean I want to dress up in spandex and beat up criminals. There are various ways to be a hero, not just the one portrayed in movies and in comic books. I wanted to be a superhero while also playing to my strengths and involving my other interests. This answer came to me in my sophomore year. It was love at first sight between my Biology course and me. Every lesson fascinated me, and I excelled in the class. Simultaneously, fear spread around the world as the Ebola virus ravaged parts of Africa and right here on my island Chikungunya and Dengue spread amongst the people. Deeply saddened, I felt this sudden need to do something about it. I could not live to disappoint the superhero-loving kid in me by not trying to help those in need through something I knew I could do. With all this, I realized what kind of superhero I wanted to be. I want to be the superhero that wears a lab coat all day and stares into microscopes, the superhero that finds out what is wrong with people and helps them get better, and the superhero that a kid like me can look up to.

# Portfolio and Video Submissions

More and more colleges are accepting extra materials as part of their application. This is especially true for schools that have begun to waive the standardized test (SAT/ACT) requirements. Anyone planning to pursue an arts degree (drama, dance, fine art, film, etc.) will often be asked to submit a portfolio or video.

*I went to lots of Portfolio Review Days and college fairs to try and learn all my options. I also went with friends who wanted to pursue an art career. Portfolio Review is something you only need to worry about if you plan to go into a creative field or a specific major that requires you to submit a portfolio with your college application. What is needed for each portfolio varies depending on the college type (private, specialized, career-oriented colleges, etc) and your desired major. Most art colleges don't have a "general application" so you have to know what major you are going into before you apply and follow the portfolio guidelines for that major.*

*On Portfolio Review Day(s), all the big art colleges get together and set up review booths where potential applicants can bring their portfolios and get feedback on what to add, remove, or how to improve a portfolio. It's basically like a college career fair but more specialized and informative to benefit each applicant's specific needs and inquiries. I highly recommend going to a Portfolio Review Day if you are planning or thinking about pursuing a career in an art field. The lines are long but the feedback is worth the time.*

—Phoenix Rose Hoffman, Laguna College of Art and Design

# Is it Optional?
# Do Your Best to Submit Materials

The goal is to help the admissions team get a more thorough picture of who you are and what makes you interesting. To that end, schools are increasingly encouraging optional, supplemental materials. If you have an online portfolio, for example, consider including a link to it if the application gives you the option.

*Schools may also advertise optional admissions opportunities through their portal, such as a video submission. For example, for Claremont McKenna, I had the option of sending in a video response to a prompt they had posted on the portal. Whenever something is optional for a college, you should always do it, especially if you really want to get into that school. Completing such tasks can give you more points of contact with your dream school and truly showcase your personality in a more wholesome way.*

—Shanaya Sidhu, UCLA

The requirements for some applications can be highly specific, the more specialized your major and the schools you target.

*The application process to Fashion Institute of Design and Merchandising (FIDM) is a lot different than your typical university because it is such a specialized private school. I had to not only write an application essay, provide recommendation letters, submit a resume, and pay the necessary application fees, but also complete a project based on the beauty industry, and finally participate in a phone interview with the head of admissions. My project was about a cosmetic brand that I created. I had to evaluate the target market, describe and explain what the various products within the brand do, as well as design the logo and packaging.*

—BAILEY RASIC, FASHION INSTITUTE OF DESIGN AND MERCHANDISING

# Auditions—Be True to Yourself!

If you are hoping to enter the theater, music, or dance program in college, the application usually includes an audition. That process differs from school to school, ranging from in-person to digital submissions. Even if you are a seasoned stage performer, the idea of laying your talent on the line for admission to your dream college can be intimidating. The following advice from a student who has been through the ordeal is wise and worth reading no matter what your major or intended career track.

GILLIAN RABIN,
OGLETHORPE UNIVERSITY
(RECIPIENT OF THE
OGLETHORPE THEATRE SCHOLARSHIP)

Auditioning for colleges began as one of the most trying periods of my life. I never really had issues with auditioning before, but the thought of going up against students from all over the country (and the world, depending on the program you are applying for) absolutely petrified me. It made me feel entirely inadequate and prompted negative thoughts to consume my confidence: my resume was not strong enough; I had not trained as much as I should have; my audition material was trite and overdone; why would they ever choose me?

These disparaging critiques did not help me whatsoever. I became tense when I performed, constricting my voice and my emotions. This tension, of course, allowed for a self-fulfilling prophecy to form; as I continued to stress over my perceived inadequacy, I felt less and less prepared for my auditions. It was not until I had a conversation with one of my best friends, who had already gone through her college auditions and wound up at the University of Central Florida's BFA Musical Theatre program, that I finally reframed my perspective. I dropped the exorbitant weight of my negative thoughts and felt instantly lighter. I began singing with more precision and support, began performing my monologues with more passion and comprehension, and began dancing with more poise and energy than ever before. Something within me switched and I was reaping the benefits of a brighter, more realistically optimistic attitude thanks to my good friend.

"Gillian, talent is only going to get you into their audition room. Beyond that, your talent is secondary to how you look and who they already have. If they already have four small blonde girls who can belt and cry on cue, they do not need you. If they have four tall brunettes with operatic voices, they need you. You cannot take it personally, Gill, or it will destroy you."

It is so simple, but so powerful. Your talent, cultivated or natural, is secondary in many cases to what the department you are auditioning for needs. The reality of this boosted my confidence to eliminate the pieces of my audition that were attempts at reaching beyond my type to show my "range" and "abilities." After that conversation, I decided to choose audition material that showcased *me*, not who I thought they wanted me to be. My repertoire changed for the better as I only chose material with which I had a deep connection. I chose one of Libby's monologues from Neil Simon's *I Ought to be in Pictures* for my contemporary auditions, one of Eliza's monologues from George Bernard Shaw's *Pygmalion* for my classic auditions, and one of Phoebe's monologues from Shakespeare's *As You Like It* for my Shakespearean auditions. These monologues all held a personal relation to me or my acting career in some way and that connection allowed me to delve into the meanings, thematics, and characterizations of the text to produce some wonderful work.

I no longer felt intimidated at my auditions. I went in with a very "if it's meant to be" attitude. I prepared to the best of my ability; I sharpened my toolset; I rehearsed my songs and my monologues until even my mother begged me to "be a little quieter, please!"; I spent hours in front of my bathroom mirror practicing blocking, facial expressions, enunciation, and other performative techniques; I honed my craft to the best of my current ability. But, once I step out of the audition room, I have done all I can do and the ultimate decision is out of my hands. I cannot alter the "type" one school's department needs nor can I alter who I am to fit it.

I felt proud of my efforts and was not offended in the slightest if I was not accepted to a program. I no longer thought, "you didn't get in because they didn't *want* you." Now, I thought, "you didn't get in because they didn't *need* you *right now*." Oglethorpe University needed me. I was in the right audition room at the right time, in the right year, and under the right circumstance. The stars aligned for *me* to go to Oglethorpe and learn, explore, and grow under the guidance of some amazing teachers. The stars may align for *you* to go somewhere else. But, wherever that "else" may be, make sure you are presenting *yourself* and not who you think they want you to be. Auditioning a false self is akin to theatrical perjury! Imagine keeping up the facade that you presented in your audition for the next four years of your life! The best auditions are those that showcase you and only you.

### How I Got into My Dream College: The Audition

Jaquez Robinson,
American Musical and Dance Academy
(AMDA)

I started looking for performing art colleges in my freshman year of high school and the first thing that popped up was this amazing school called American Musical and Dramatic Academy known as AMDA.

During my sophomore year I went to New York City for the first time, and I suggested to my parents that we visit AMDA. I loved the city lights, and the Broadway strip was truly magnificent. It definitely was the city that never sleeps. Attending AMDA's open house was better than I ever expected. It exceeded my wildest dreams. I was able to meet alumnus Kyle Scatliffe who was the lead in *Les Miserables*, and he explained his journey of becoming a Broadway actor. I was able to tour the school and perform in a sample dance screening. The goal of the open house was for us to see all aspects of the school. I knew that this would be the school I would work so hard to try to get into. I needed to go to a college that only focused on arts. I wanted to only be surrounded by peers who loved their craft. I didn't know how I would be able to go to this college but I knew I would find a way to achieve this major goal.

From this point on all I cared about was AMDA. I auditioned for a performing arts high school named Capital Area School for the Arts and was able to get in the theatre department. I was overwhelmed with excitement because to me this put me one step closer to my dream college. I attended Capital Area School for the Arts Charter School, known as CASA to continue to pursue my passion for theatre. A few months later I saw on AMDA's website that I could apply for early acceptance to college as a junior in high school. I immediately told my mother, and she found a location in Philadelphia where I could audition. My theatre teacher, Robert Campbell, helped me prepare my monologue for my audition, and my parents took me to a few voice lessons for my musical theatre song.

After all the training to prepare me for audition, we drove to Philadelphia for my audition to get into the musical theatre program. I had so many emotions running through my brain and body. I signed in, watched a quick video on AMDA, and met some of the most interesting and most talented group of students I have ever met. I was truly amazed to see that most of the students came from faraway places just to get a chance to audition for this amazing school. Some were from Florida, France, Russia, Texas, and Beijing, and their stories truly amazed. Waiting in line I could hear the students singing or acting. Their voices were incredible and their acting had so much passion. I remember thinking to myself as each one left the room "I bet that he was born to do this. He is going to make it in." For a moment I doubted myself, then I remember how I got here and the people who helped me get here and this is something that I want to do. Failure wasn't an option I knew this college was for me. I would walk into that room confident and give them the best version of myself. I was nervous, of course. But the moment I went into the audition room, heard the music play, and started my monologue, I felt more engaged on that stage than I had been in a long time. Afterwards I had to sit with an administrator of the school and explain why I should be chosen to attend AMDA. When the audition was totally complete, the waiting process began. I had to wait four weeks for a response.

A few weeks went by, and, to be honest, I really didn't think that I would make it in. I mean, I had to sit in the room with some of the most talented and experienced students that I had ever met. Then I would tell myself, "Jaquez, you got this." It was the longest four weeks of my life. One night I was asleep in my room when my dad woke me up and told me to go up to my Nana's house with him and my mom. I was kind of nervous because they didn't tell me exactly why we were going. Once we got to my grandparents' house and went through the greetings, my Nana said she wanted to show me something on her computer. I was not thinking about college; I was just trying to figure out what could be on her computer. I went along with what she said and we all walked into her office. She told me to close my eyes and not to open them until she said, so I was nervous. When she told me to open my eyes I saw a black and white video from the administrator of AMDA saying that she loved my audition and that I got accepted to attend the American Musical and Dramatic Academy. That moment was the best; I ran and screamed and cried. It was the best moment of my life. I was in complete shock seeing the video and then my Nana played it again because I couldn't believe it was real. She then showed me my acceptance letter.

There was so much emotion that day realizing that I got accepted to not only my number one college choice but to one of the best musical theatre colleges ever. I felt complete. I thought, "I am a junior in high school and I have been accepted to college." I realized that my acceptance into college from AMDA was the start of a new journey This would be the journey of my life. This showed me I could do anything. However, I didn't think this was the end, this was just the beginning. I now need to work twice as hard if I ever want to make it in the theatre business. I need to eat and sleep music. The acceptance letter was the beginning of my life.

# The Guidance and Influence of Others on Your Journey

In telling his story of getting into his dream performing arts school, Jaquez touches on an important factor—that there were many people who helped him achieve his goal. Parents, grandparents, teachers, and even his talented competition helped him hone his skills and stay focused on his goal. Here is another student story that adeptly points to the support, guidance, honesty, and inspiration that the people around him provided.

MY JOURNEY TO YALE

SELAH BELL,
YALE UNIVERSITY

This isn't going to be a step-by-step guideline that'll gift you with a guaranteed path into your dream school. No walkthrough, however detailed and intricate, can promise you that. While it's true that you can search "How do I get into X university" and Google will spit out seemingly endless amalgams of answers, there's really no way of telling if those answers will apply to you. Everyone's college acceptance story is unique. Instead of bombarding you with statistics and specific steps I'll share a condensed version of my story. Any advice I provide will be legitimized by my own personal experiences and journey. This journey was grounded in a clear and focused mindset that was shaped by the people around me.

When you and your family begin thinking about college applications the first thing you need to focus on is clearing your mind. At many points I felt so bombarded by the information, options, offers, and conflicting expectations surrounding me, that for a while I couldn't figure out where I truly wanted to go. Going into my junior year, I constantly reflected on what kind of experience I wanted for myself in college. This would have been in a constant state of flux if it weren't for the influence and guidance of specific members of my community.

## Mr. Hunt

For a while, all I could think about was basketball. It fueled my competitive spirit and excited me in ways few other activities could. It didn't matter how sad, frustrated, or anxious I felt, once I had a ball in my hand I couldn't help but smile. My junior year was my breakout season and I was convinced that I should pursue basketball in college. I was so ready to put everything else to the side, blinded by highlights of college players soaring, diving, and getting cheered on by thousands. But Mr. Hunt brought me back to reality. Mr. Hunt was my history teacher for a year and then my coach for my last two years of high school. He had a reputation as someone who was both witty and stern; there'd be no sugar coating from him yet he was also sure to make you laugh. As a coach he instilled a disciplined and systematic approach to the game. He adored defense, grit, and the fundamentals. But I fell in love with the game for its grace and flashiness. We naturally butted heads and had plenty of disputes in his classroom about how the team should play. Despite that, I ended up thriving in his system and was convinced that I should consider playing in college. As the season came to a close I worked up the nerve to ask him what he thought my chances were of playing D1 in the U.S. I was sure he'd say I could at least be a role player for a lower tier D1 school, but no. He believed I still had some ways to go if I wanted to start on a D2 or D3 team. I was crushed. Yet it was the best thing I could have heard. Although I loved basketball, I didn't train and play as hard or as often as most American prospects. They practiced every day, had yearlong seasons, and sacrificed almost everything for the sport. If I wanted to reach that level I'd have to change my whole life, prioritizing basketball over school, extra curricular work, and sleep; it was hard to accept but I knew that wasn't for me. Thanks to Mr. Hunt's words, I recognized that I wasn't going to be a student athlete, and was able to pour my all into my studies and community service. I still played ball and was even the captain in my senior year. But I didn't let that fool me into thinking basketball would be my ticket to a great school.

Mr. Hunt's brutal honesty played a key role in the process of my college application essay too. A couple of weeks into school I had finished editing and drafting the essay, answering a prompt about failure. It was a safe and admittedly conventional essay, yet I had high hopes until the day I let Mr. Hunt look at it. When I came by the next morning he went over some potential improvements I could make. But as I was leaving his classroom he stopped me, saying "if you're trying to get into an Ivy League, this isn't gonna cut it." All I could do was let out a nervous laugh, assuming he meant that I had a lot more edits to make. But that wasn't it. He wanted me to scrap the essay and come back with an entirely new idea tackling a different prompt. That's the last thing I wanted to hear and it took a lot for me to begin drafting countless ideas again for the next couple of nights. Part of me wanted to just go back to the first essay; surely if I spent enough time on it I could perfect it and prove my coach wrong. This exchange felt like the college basketball one all over again. In simple terms, neither I, nor my essay, was good enough. I saw exactly what he did. My essay was mediocre. It was predictable; the type of story an admissions officer would read hundreds of times every year. I had to adapt, and with the aid of someone else in my life I was able to do just that.

### Tshepo

The second time around I knew I had to tackle an idea or present a concept that distinguished me from other applicants. If I didn't grab the attention of whoever was reading my application within the first few sentences, they'd be unlikely to get through the whole piece. I realized I had to present the type of story an admissions officer would find refreshing, one that would make them pay keen attention to my entire application. I was determined that my essay wouldn't be a chore. I would share something memorable.

For some context, between 2005 and 2016 I grew up in Johannesburg, South Africa. There, I was able to compete in a club basketball league once my high school season ended. I also did a lot of community service in the townships near my school, Diepsloot and Alexandria.

Central to my essay was my basketball rival and then teammate, Tshepo. I knew our relationship was unique and special, one definitely worth discussing. My essay explored our differences, our shared passion for basketball, and how working together in Alexandria, one of South Africa's toughest slums, could positively impact our community. Tshepo was an orphan tasked with finishing high school and taking care of his younger sister. We got to know each other by initially competing in club basketball. However, we also worked together on a fundraiser connected to the service I was doing in his community alongside an organization called Afrika Tikkun. This culminated in a shoe drive fundraiser I ran. That aside, Afrika Tikkun's work focused on development in underprivileged slums through education, sports, and job readiness programs. Together with some other students from school I carried out a weekly basketball clinic for kids there; we would teach them the fundamentals of the game and hone some social skills they could make use of at school or at home. The organization was significant because it kept vulnerable kids/teens engaged in productive and worthwhile activities. Rather than being exposed to potentially enticing yet dangerous influences existing in between their homes and school, they were in a supervised, safe, and enlightening space.

This community service work along with my essay really helped my application in several ways. First, it demonstrated that I had a genuine appreciation and care for the broader South African community. Many expats tend to coalesce into a bubble of similar middle to upper class foreigners. This especially includes the high school students, who will engage in the mandatory community service hours without taking things a step further—I had friends in that extended community, through basketball and service, with whom I shared memorable experiences. However, that friendship also allowed me to expand the beneficial reach of the service work I was doing. It's so easy to get completely absorbed into school life. You can forget that you are part of a city or town that has other people living in it who are heavily affected by your actions and the actions of your school. It's one thing to be aware of that. But it is another to act on it to make tangible differences in the lives of aforementioned people. By talking about my fundraiser and Tshepo I showed a part of who I am and what my core values are, aspects of myself that I know universities could appreciate. This also helped my application as it displayed a self-awareness of the privilege that I have. I reflected on how lucky I was to have the opportunities that I did, opportunities that others, who were just as deserving, were not afforded. Finally, by end of my essay I tried to come away from everything with a general life lesson that I can apply elsewhere. I wanted the university to know that wasn't just a coincidental event I let happen to me, but rather something that helped shape who I was and would allow me to do similar or greater things once further empowered by the university. None of this would have been possible without Tshepo. My relationship with him gave me a means to do meaningful community service that I was passionate about. It also provided me a friend, who's tough perspective kept me humbled and grateful for the life I've been able to have so far.

## Mrs. van Niekerk & Dr. Kissack

There were two other teachers at my school who helped cement my idea of where I wanted to go after college, albeit in a very different way than Mr. Hunt. Mrs. van Niekerk was my English teacher and Extended Essay advisor (the extended essay is a quasi-independent research paper students have to complete in the IB). She also coached me for a year when I experimented with cross-country. By my senior year she was clearly my favorite teacher and the one I could be my most open and honest self with. We especially bonded over our shared obsession with the author Haruki Murakami. What I appreciated most about Mrs. Van Niekerk was her desire to see me become the best possible version of myself. The care that she had for me was most manifested in the detailed and enriching feedback she provided me during the Extended Essay process. I'll never forget how patient and faithful she was, encouraging me to formulate complex ideas and arguments that I didn't know I was capable of creating. She pushed me out of my comfort zone and forced me to recognize the need to keep challenging myself in writing.

Another teacher I was captivated by was Dr. Kissack. He taught History and Theory of Knowledge, the latter of which being the class in which I had the most endearing and enlightening experience. His teaching style relied on students' willingness to participate and discuss matters at length with him throughout the class. We students were initially intimidated by this, as we covered material that appeared very abstract and convoluted. None of us felt smart enough to be going back and forth about such complicated ideas. It took a while for me to view Dr. Kissack's knowledge and intelligence as a means through which I could smoothly acquaint myself with all of this complex information. It wasn't about being smart enough, but rather humble enough to acknowledge one's ignorance, make mistakes, and to ask 'dumb' questions (that literally everyone else in the class is thinking). There was so much I could gain from his insight, but only if I was willing to risk sounding a little confused. Dr. Kissack was visibly surprised when, after the first week, I was suddenly more vocal and inquisitive about everything. As the semester continued I found myself staying after class to keep the conversation going, ever appreciative of how generous this man was to impart such wisdom and guidance onto me. I never would have reached that point of comfort and genuine curiosity if I hadn't first risked embarrassment and judgment by engaging in class discussions early on. Dr. Kissack expressed gratitude for me doing this too, acknowledging my effort and contribution to the class.

My experiences with Mrs. van Niekerk and Dr. Kissack gave me essential writing and discussion tools that served me well in the application process. I still benefit from those tools today. However, they also helped me realize that I'd benefit the most from a school that had a low student to faculty ratio and many seminars. Before becoming so engaged with those two, I didn't realize how valuable that personalized learning experience was for me. If I was to make the most of college, I'd need to interact directly with my professors and be comfortable enough to vocalize my concerns. Smaller schools offer more opportunities for this. Fortunately, connecting with them the way I did made my two teachers ideal for writing recommendation letters too. Both had a reliable sense of the type of student and person I was.

## Mom

I am fortunate to have a mom that sets high, realistic standards. She is focused on people challenging themselves and growing. Several hours outside a deadline I remember my mom ruthlessly critiquing an essay and making me rewrite several paragraphs. At the time I was so exasperated with her. We'd go back and forth about the way a sentence was worded. I didn't understand why there always seemed to be something I had to change and improve after so many rounds of review. Whenever we got to the end though I'd always be overcome with a wave of embarrassment and gratefulness. She was always right and, like Mrs. van Niekerk, would pull the best out of me by any means necessary.

Thus, unsurprisingly, my mom was dead set on me either going to an Ivy League school or somewhere comparable. Anywhere else and she was convinced that I wouldn't be challenging myself. Anything merely satisfactory wasn't enough; I had to go above and beyond. As a black woman in America she had no choice but to work 10 times smarter and harder than her peers to get the same type of recognition and benefits. Although America has progressed since she was my age she still knows that there's no way I could be successful and achieve what I wanted to just by being average. She was well aware of the sort of doors that would be opened and the privileges that'd be afforded to me if I was to get into an Ivy League. The elitism of it all does bother me, especially when I meet or hear about kids who are just as smart and hardworking as me if not more who miss out on opportunities like this because of a lack of people in their corner. That often holds them back.

To continue, my mom is my biggest advocate. She often believes in me more than I believe in myself. Initially, I thought Ivy leagues were out of reach and my counselor felt the same way. My mom was on the complete opposite end of the spectrum; we had to convince her to even let me apply to more than one safety school (a term she detests). Without her I never would have realized my potential. "Selah this won't happen if you don't have your mind right. Speak it into existence and believe it," she'd repeat whenever she sensed any serious doubt festering within me. I was amazed and frustrated at how stubbornly faithful she was. This faith was unwavering, so I had no choice but to trust her.

## Yale

I ended up applying to Boston College, Harvard, University of California (Berkeley), USC, Cornell, University of Virginia, and Yale. I was interested in the field of natural resource management and environmental studies; Yale had the most endearing environmental studies concentration by far. But visiting Yale was what cemented it as my new dream school. Towards the end of my junior summer my mom and I went on a college tour to various schools on the East Coast (UPenn, Harvard, Yale, and Boston College). Yale had the biggest impression on me as it shattered many of my presumptions about it. I expected the people and atmosphere to come across as uptight, preppy, and entitled. In hindsight, these were some dumb and rash assumptions I had. They stemmed more from what I'd seen on TV and my own insecurities rather than anything experiential. In reality, the people I met were all excited and appreciative, exuding a contagious sense of eagerness. The campus itself was a lot more beautiful than I expected too. Part of its allure was because of the school's commitment to sustainability. The building housing its School of Forestry and Environmental Studies, called Kroon Hall, was powered by solar panels and a functioning geothermal plant. I loved that I could see the school being accountable and demonstrating the principles it valued. By then, I was sure that it was a place where I could contribute and thrive. I quickly developed a strong desire to become a part of the university. Yale evoked an enthusiasm that no other school could compare to, and eventually lead me to apply Early Decision and get accepted.

My mindset was a determining factor in all of this. It set what I prioritized in high school, who I surrounded myself with, what I valued in my learning experience, and ultimately what school I wanted to attend. But on top of that, a solid unwavering support system is a non-negotiable. Your support system is essential to jumping all the hurdles in the college application process. If the support system isn't within your immediate family, set out to find it elsewhere. Be relentless, you will need people to push you when you want to give up and people who will let you know that you can do better. No matter how trying that gets it'll bring out the best within you. Mr. Hunt, Tshepo, Dr. Kissack, Mrs. van Niekerk, and my Mom were imperative to me being where I am today.

## My Application Essay

I knew I had to tackle an idea or present a concept that distinguished me from other applicants. If I didn't grab the attention of whoever was reading my application within the first few sentences, they'd be unlikely to get through the whole piece. I realized I had to present the type of story an admissions officer would find refreshing, one that would make them pay keen attention to my entire application. I was determined that my essay wouldn't be a chore. I would share something memorable. Not only was my relationship with Tshepo memorable, but it was reflective of a lot my personal values and the way I exercised those values while living in South Africa.

Another shot splashed through the net and the crowd roared, he just could not miss. His mystic hands guided the ball through the defense as if it was spellbound, and I found myself cheering along with everyone else in a wave of admiration. With torn shoes and an unorthodox style, Tshepo managed to regularly leave his defenders inept. His eyes burned with a strong passion to simply play. That mesmerizing fire enriched my own love for the game of basketball.

I met Tshepo, an orphan from the Alexandra Township, through a city basketball league where we were first fierce opponents and then harmonious teammates. On the court we meshed as his loose style rubbed off on me while my disciplined mindset influenced him. We could talk for hours about a game we just played, breaking down every minute detail of our performances, and that is where he always reminded me of the importance of self-evaluation over self-glorification. He noted that even in games as great as the one I first saw him play in, there is always something to improve. In his mind, there was no such thing as a perfect game or a perfect life, a tough yet rewarding reality.

Despite his inherent burdens, I saw a lot of myself in Tshepo; it was as if we were on two sides of the same coin. I would always find myself questioning why this kid, somewhat a reflection of myself, had to be the one stripped of all the things that make my life so privileged. It was gripping and humbling, I felt as if I could so easily have been in his position. At first that frightened me, and caused me to stray away from him, but soon I realized that my biggest failure would be completely losing grasp of Tshepo; getting caught up in the material world rather than improving my tangible one. That was when I remembered Tshepo's torn shoes on the court, like many youth in Alexandra, he played in whatever he could find, at times leaving him barefoot. How could I make a difference?

The viability of a shoe drive struck me; I had shoes I outgrew, shoes donated by family friends, and shoes from students at my school, and so began *NMyShoes* an initiative to collect and distribute quality footwear for underprivileged basketball players. After every donation, I clearly saw the difference shoes made. The players suddenly displayed improved confidence in their game, and began to assume impactful roles on their teams. The value and impact of *NMyShoes* was confirmed. It also emphasized the connectivity I had with Tshepo's life; I felt somewhat responsible for him. Suddenly, out of nowhere, everything changed. I could not find Tshepo. His circumstances proved to be too overwhelming and we were separated. However, I still felt like I was a part of his world, the township. One day I would be surrounded by a group of guys doing the one thing they love without a care in the world, and the next I would be back in school, enveloped by the egos, the drama, and the tenacious workload. It was difficult to understand how these two worlds fit together, until I understood that I was the missing piece. Tshepo's absence stung, yet his words managed to persist in my mind; self-evaluation over self-glorification.

I recognized my opportunity to take advantage of what I gained from both worlds, and now sport a strong resolve to create and maintain connections between communities in need and my higher education. Tshepo's presence and absence in my life and the experiences I have had with *NMyShoes* have molded my approach to the difficulties of being caught between two unique worlds. My goal is to leave Johannesburg with a durable bridge joining the two together.

# Overcoming Challenges

Many of the student stories describe situations in which the individuals have overcome significant challenges in order to achieve their goals. In doing so, these students have learned to approach obstacles with a mindset that is inherently open to positive outcomes. Fear, failure, language barriers, economic hardships, competition, illness, and injury are viewed as character-building realities, not excuses. With big dreams in mind, these students persevere with grit and grace. You can too!

### HOW I GOT INTO MY DREAM COLLEGE

RIMPAL BAJWA,
GEORGETOWN UNIVERSITY

Growing up in a small suburb, I always heard about how kids from our town weren't destined to make it. We were instructed to dream small so our hearts wouldn't be broken when we received our inevitable rejection letters. Fear of failure was instilled within us, stopping us from ever trying to even pursue our dreams. We watched as talent after talent failed to get into the college of their dreams, further reinforcing the notion that the kids from our small town were doomed to the same fate of rejection. But I had the audacity to dream. Because I was not scared of failure or rejection, I was scared of never even trying to chase my dreams. Although I didn't know it at the time, my journey of getting into the college of my dreams started when I was in elementary school. Growing up in a traditional Indian household, I was surrounded by Punjabi, unfamiliar with the language of English. At school, my teacher recognized my incompetency in English and placed me in English as a Second Language (ESL). I dedicated countless hours to learning a language that came naturally to the ones around me. I failed, persevered, and finally succeeded. The next year, I was placed into QUEST, a program for highly gifted elementary students. Instead of falling behind in school like before, I had accelerated ahead by overcoming the language barrier that existed between my teachers and me.

Overcoming the challenges I faced in ESL didn't just help me learn English, it helped me construct a mindset of determination and persistence, one that shaped the way I would approach school for years to come. My placement into QUEST meant that I could enter the PAGE program in junior high, an accelerated program for gifted kids. In seventh grade, I made a list of colleges I wanted to go to, all of which were the most difficult schools to get into. Of course, the list was at best a rough draft of the colleges I wanted to apply to but it still showed me that I had an ambitious goal in front of me.

My peers always thought my parents had set the high expectations I always pursued, but in reality, I had set those for myself. I was intrinsically motivated, not extrinsically motivated and that made all the difference. At the tender age of 13, I understood that the margin of error was very small for me, considering that I started taking classes that would go on my high school transcript in seventh grade. I watched as my peers succumbed to the distractions of high school, trying my best to not let my focus waver. Education in the U.S. is often taken for granted but I knew to never overlook the opportunities I had been gifted and the sacrifices my parents had made for me. Being a first-generation American didn't automatically give me an edge on my peers in college admissions, it was my determination to never take my opportunities for granted.

So, I began the journey to find myself in junior high. I became involved with community service, band, volleyball, and leadership; desperately trying to find what passion I would channel to propel me forward. At the end of junior high, I found that serving the community and simultaneously being a leader in it was what I was most genuinely passionate about. I was determined to carry that passion with me throughout my life, which is why I joined as many community service clubs as I could in high school, such as Key Club, Health Occupations Students of America, Family, Career, Community Leaders of America, Viking Lady, eventually earning leadership positions in all of the aforementioned clubs. Over the span of four years, I accumulated over 1,000 hours of community service and helped cultivate an atmosphere of sharing and giving in my school.

While I had not chosen what college was my number one on my list, the hardest one to get in to, at the time, was Harvard University. I knew that if I strove to get into the hardest university and met all their requirements, I could build a resume capable of impressing almost any college. I found a list of recommended AP courses on the Harvard website and took as many of them as I could throughout the course of high school. In total, I took 11 AP courses and earned the AP Scholar with Distinction honor from College Board. I also noticed that most rigorous colleges recommended taking SAT subject tests, along with the SAT and ACT, encouraging me to take multiple of them to present on my resume. While all these tests seemed to consume all my time, I refused to let my high school career be defined by only academics and standardized tests, which is why I joined two career-oriented clubs, Debate and Distributive Education Clubs of America, to help me develop skills that would prove to be useful in the future.

Debate and DECA were easily the highlights of my high school career. In DECA, I competed in business law and qualified for state in that category two years in a row. As a senior, I was given the responsibility to manage the school espresso bar and write a manual about it, which ultimately qualified for Nationals. In Debate, I competed in public forum and original oratory, allowing me to refine both my argumentative and speaking skills. But debating didn't just boost my resume; it introduced me to topics I would've never been exposed to otherwise. I went from debating whether Catalonia deserved independence to advocating for whether NCAA players deserve to be paid, allowing me to develop educated stances on controversial topics. I debated in the cold freezing winter at Harvard, in the blistering heat at UNLV, and under the palm trees at Stanford. I told the story of my family struggling to maintain their cultural identity and fight conformity at the national tournament in Denver, ultimately being recognized as being one of the Top 60 speakers in the nation. At the National Speech and Debate Tournament in Florida, my debate team placed as the Top 50 in the nation. Thanks to Debate, I went from being a shy girl to being an empowered woman with plenty of local and national recognition under her belt. But more importantly, I learned that I had a voice that could initiate change. On March 14, 2018, I, with my fellow debate co-captain, led a group of students out of school, marching in remembrance for the lives lost in the Parkland shooting. Through Debate, I managed to cultivate and polish my skill of public speaking, allowing me to convey my opinions and beliefs with confidence. Fighting for your rights, whether it's the right to live or the right to bear arms, is something I learned I was passionate about, which is why I determined that in the future, I want to be an international human rights lawyer.

With this career choice in mind, I finally realized the perfect college for me: Georgetown University. Located in the political heart of the nation, Georgetown University has arguably the best international relations program in the country: the Walsh School of Foreign Service. Knowing that I wanted to major in international relations helped me narrow down my list significantly, which is why it is important for applicants to keep in mind what they want to get out of their degree and to see if the college they're looking at actually provides it. I knew that it would be extremely difficult to gain admission at such a prestigious college but I also knew that the resume I had built throughout the past six years was competitive enough to gain their attention. But I knew it was more than just my past activities and awards; it was about how well I could get my application to encapsulate who I truly was. I spent weeks writing, editing, then re-editing my personal essay, seeking help from peers and teachers. Countless students applying to rigorous colleges have impressive test scores and grades but colleges want to see writing that stick out from the rest. Writing comes from the soul and fabricated lies are so easy to see through, which is why when you write, you want to write your truth.

Sometimes colleges provide applicants with a variety of prompts to choose from, which is something the student can use to their advantage. When carefully selecting a prompt, it is important to remember that colleges want to see you describe who you are as a person not just as a student, so picking a prompt that allows you to elaborate on your background and how your goals came to be is always a great idea. Some questions to remember are: What can you give to the college that no one else can give? What will motivate you even when times get rough? What struggles have you endured that made you a more resilient person? I kept all these questions in mind while completing the college application process. Along with Georgetown University, I applied to University of California, Berkeley; University of California, Los Angeles; Harvard University; New York University; Fordham University; and University of Southern California.

College applications usually follow the same format, which includes answering basic personal questions, listing activities and honors, and completing essay prompts. Of course, it is important to have diverse activities to show on the application but it is also essential to have something to show for how you excelled at that activity. Because of this, it is very important to understand what the requirements for varsity letters are early on. I got a varsity letter from every club that I could earn it from, sometimes even lettering multiple years in those activities; I lettered three times in Key Club and DECA, and twice in HOSA and Debate. I even earned varsity letters from outside organizations, such as the varsity letters from United Way for community service and varsity letters from Puyallup School District for community service as well. When looking at honors on the application, colleges are really impressed when they see an applicant has national recognition, which is why it is helpful for an applicant to seek out ways to get onto a national platform. An applicant receiving other scholarships also shows the college that other organizations find the student worthy of receiving money to pursue a college education, which is why it helps if the student starts applying for scholarships as early as junior year.

Some colleges that I had applied required interviews, a step I was very excited about. Both Debate and DECA had forced me to develop sophisticated social skills, allowing me to gracefully present myself in a social situation. I looked up interview tips beforehand but found myself getting anxious at all the information online. Some people had pleasant experiences with their interviews while others had a less than great time. To prevent myself from getting overwhelmed, I decided to not study questions and formulate complete answers beforehand. Instead, I decided that I would provide genuine answers to the questions my interviewer asked me to allow them to truly see if I was a perfect fit for their university. For me, that strategy worked great because I was able to relax and openly communicate with my interviewer, allowing the conversation to be more natural and informal. However, I think interview strategies vary greatly with each applicant because not everyone behaves the same in social situations. I do encourage applicants to just brainstorm what they could talk about beforehand so they can communicate their answers in an effective manner. It is important to take interviews seriously though because interviewers report back on whether or not the applicants would be a nice addition to the college culture.

But there is more to the college application process than just the applicant's contributions. Throughout high school, it is very important to also make connections with the educators and administration around you. Teacher recommendation letters are extremely helpful at providing an outside perspective at the applicant's personality and characteristics, helping colleges understand how the applicant stands out from their peers. When asking for recommendation letters, I personally went in to talk to my selected teachers, asking them politely to take time out of their busy schedules to write about why they think colleges should want me. The teachers I had selected were ones that I had thought truly knew me, which is why I trusted them to speak about my attributes. It is essential to understand that teachers are not required to write students recommendations letters, which is why it is vital to showcase your gratitude. It is also helpful to connect with your counselor and speak about your college goals, helping them understand what you might need during college application season. One of the main reasons I managed to meet application deadlines is my open communication with my teachers and counselors, allowing me to constantly remind them of what needed to be completed by when. This also forced me to become more responsible because I was forced to make sure that my teachers and I met deadlines.

My piece of advice for anyone wanting to get into his or her dream college is this: if you really want it, go get it. Don't get distracted by what your peers are doing or look to an adult figure to tell you what to do with your life. Take initiative and do the research to get the college of your dreams to notice you. But don't lose yourself in the process; stay true to who you are because once you find your passion, it will motivate you beyond all other measures to chase your dream and stay focused. High school is full of opportunities so make the most of them to ensure that you are not missing out on something that you could potentially enjoy. Try to find something that helps you stand out from your peers in some way, whether it be in the community, athletically, academically, or as a leader. Use your talent or even your raw passion to make some change in your community because colleges are look-ing for the future leaders that aren't afraid to challenge the status quo. But also, make sure the college you want to go to is truly the college of your dreams and not one that you want to go to for the prestige or recognition. Match your future goals and personality to your pre-sumed dream college and assess your compatibility. In the end, it's important to recognize that an acceptance or rejection letter won't drastically alter your future unless you let it. Rejection, at some point in life, is inevitable, which is why you have to build your self-esteem up to the point where you are confident in your abilities yet still aware of your own flaws. College is a stepping-stone to the future, not the future itself.

# What If You Still Have Questions?

All of the examples in this book are meant to provide reassurance, guidance, and hope, but there is no way to cover every situation here. Chances are, you will have questions and need to ask for help. Remember that your teachers, guidance counsel-ors, parents, coaches, siblings and friends who have been through the process might be able to offer general help. When you have school-specific questions, however, it's time to reach out to the admissions counselors directly.

*When you need to contact the school you are applying to, be it for random questions, urgent problems, or anything in between, nothing beats a human conversation! Send emails to the appropriate offices to document your request, but the fastest way to get the information you need is to call the office directly. The people who work in the offices are always happy to help, and they are often current students who you can ask about their experiences. Don't be afraid to pick up the phone to call, because it guarantees your request won't get lost in a void of emails.*

—MAILE HARRIS, YALE UNIVERSITY

# You've Submitted Your Applications, Now What?

What a relief! You should be proud of all your hard work and the care that you took in applying to the college(s) of your dreams. Waiting for the results can be brutal, but there some proactive things you can do in the meantime.

*Once I turned in all of my applications, then it was time to just wait for the decisions. Make sure you create accounts through your colleges' portals. This is where important information is posted about additional documents you may be required to send in and your eventual admissions decision. Colleges will email you about how to set up these portals, and you should set them up as soon as you get these emails. Colleges will also email you when there is a 'status update' in your portal, which usually means your admissions decision is up. While your applications are under review, I would highly recommend visiting the schools you applied to, contacting the schools, and exploring your options more. Nowadays, colleges keep track of how many times you contact them, which can play a factor in your admissions. Colleges love when you contact them and display interest, and this is something I wish I had done more of after I turned in my applications. You should also keep an eye out for scholarships offered through the schools you applied to. They will usually email you about such opportunities, and it is in your best interest to apply.*

—SHANAYA SIDHU, UCLA

Be sure to keep your senior year grades up because colleges will see them!

## Oops!

If you hit the submit button and realize you made a mistake, don't panic.

*I found that talking with your admittance counselors from the schools you applied to is the most helpful. They are experts on the application process for that school. In all of my applications, I mistyped my Social Security Number (I used the Common Application) and had to change it for every single school so I reached out to the admissions counselors at each and they directed me on how to fix it. I went to them for any questions I had and they were so helpful, so don't be afraid to reach out to them. They're there to help make the application process easier and answer any questions. Many schools also have an option for applicants to ask current students questions about what life is like on campus, which is another source to take advantage of.*

—Natalie Chandler, Baylor University

# Stay Positive and Believe in Yourself!

Lauren Campbell,
University of California, Los Angeles (UCLA)

If I could revisit the entire college application journey again and change one thing, it would be the faith I had in myself. Throughout the process, I had a lot of doubts, and a lot of anxiety. I worried my SAT scores were not high enough, and that my writing was not strong enough. I worried that ultimately *I* was not enough. I wish I had more confidence and courage. In fact, I wish I *had* decided to apply to Harvard because why not? A 5-6% acceptance rate may not be incredibly high but you never know. I had believed

UCLA was essentially impossible to get into. Throughout high school, I watched incredibly qualified people get rejected from this very school and so I thought, "If they could not do it, how could I?" I would go back and change this mentality. Thankfully, UCLA and in fact nine other schools saw something in me that I did not see in myself at the time of my application. Thus, the one burning piece of advice I would give to future students anxious over universities, acceptance rates, and selectivity is that your chances of getting in automatically go up once you send in an application. You are not guaranteed an acceptance anywhere, but you are entitled to trying. Do not put yourself down, doubt yourself or allow others to do so. I oftentimes think back to that day in December upon meeting with my high school counselor, consumed with fear as she worriedly informed me of the selectivity of the California schools I applied to, and reflect that in the end I ended up being accepted to every one of those schools. I am so incredibly thankful for this truth, and glad that I was not scared into not trying. Last year, believing UCLA could not possibly accept me after the people I have personally known them to reject, I almost did not apply, Had I not, I would have missed the opportunity to attend a remarkable university with me "written all over it." Simply put, what I am trying to say is, you never know until you try. As cliché as it sounds, it is the truth. At least, it was my truth.

# Paying for It All!

## Financial Aid and Scholarships

Paying for college is no easy task. Tuition rates are sky high, making the advertised prices out of reach for all but the wealthiest families. You should know, however, that students received more than $123.8 billion in scholarships and grants in 2014-15, according to CollegeBoard. About 37% of this free money comes from the federal government and, to qualify, you need to fill out the Free Application for Federal Student Aid, commonly referred to as the FAFSA.

The general advice from school aid officers is that you should not let the sticker price deter you from applying. Schools want a diverse student mix and that includes economic diversity as well.

The Net Price Calculator is now on every college website and can help take some of the mystery out of the college cost equation. Once you enter your information, it will tell you your Expected Family Contribution (EFC) at that school. While it is only giving you a "ballpark" idea of what you and your family will be expected to pay, it should be fairly accurate. The formula takes the sticker price of the college, subtracts estimates for any gift aid you may expect to receive, and gives you the net cost—what your family will pay using savings, loans, and income. If your EFC is

$50,000 to over $60,000, you probably won't get much, if any, need-based financial aid. Even so, there are still plenty of scholarships out there.

> A major piece of advice I would like to share with high school students—specifically those of a low household income—is to not be deterred from applying to college, due to finances. Students of a lower financial bracket thankfully receive a generous amount of financial aid—enough to pay for the majority of a student's tuition and room and board. This is especially true at private universities (i.e. Stanford, Notre Dame, Harvard, USC), since they have larger endowments.
>
> —KEVIN QUALLS, UNIVERSITY OF SOUTHERN CALIFORNIA (CLASS OF 2018); BROWN UNIVERSITY (GRADUATE STUDENT)

> In all that I have ever done during my college search and application process, the greatest regret I had was not applying for more scholarships earlier on. I was so focused on getting accepted to a college, I had totally neglected to factor in the need for financial security to pay off my college expenses. I had been told time and time again that as long as I looked for them, there were scholarships everywhere just ripe for the taking. I had underestimated this truth, and now deeply regret not having applied to more scholarships sooner.
>
> My lasting piece of advice to anyone beginning their college search and application process would be to apply to as many scholarships as possible as early in the game as you can. Because even if one were to get accepted into one's desired college, it'd be crushing to be unable to attend because of financial circumstances. Some may actually have the financial means to pay off college tuition, but I'd still recommend applying to scholarships, because there are other expenses not included in tuition and rooming that cost quite a great deal, such as books and supplies.
>
> —ABBIGAL MAENG, AUSTIN COLLEGE

If you're interested in learning how to get scholarships in high school to help pay for college, then you're making a very smart investment of your time. Getting an early start in applying for scholarships while in high school can dramatically increase your chances of earning more money to help pay for college. In turn, you can significantly reduce the overall cost of your college tuition.

Whether you're a high school senior or a forward-thinking freshman, it's never too late (or too early) to start pinpointing scholarships worth applying for. Here are a few tips to help you **find relevant and attainable scholarships to help you pay for college.**

## Start with FAFSA

For college-bound high school students based in the U.S., one of the most well-known places to start is the Free Application for Federal Student Aid (FAFSA). By submitting your FAFSA forms, you can see the financial aid that you qualify for, including scholarships, federal grants, state grants, campus-based aid, and low-interest student loans. The FAFSA application opens on October 1 for the following academic year.

Whether through Federal Pell Grants, State Grants, or scholarships, most packages will offer some amount of free aid, especially if you demonstrate financial need. Since grants and scholarships do not require repayment, exhaust these options before applying for loans through FAFSA or other private lenders. The more effort you put forth now in getting all the federal funding you can, the less overwhelming your student loan debt will be after you graduate.

Student debt is a huge and growing issue. It's important to think carefully about the debt you are willing to take on in relation to the expected income of the profession you will likely go into. If you need $65,000 in student loans, you could be paying off that debt for 20 or 30 years unless you are in a high-paying profession.

## Find Local Scholarships

Unlike some private scholarships in which hundreds and thousands of students are applying for, local scholarships are often far more attainable. A good first place to start is to check with your high school's guidance counselor. If organizations are smart, one of the first places they will promote their scholarship is through counselors in the high school guidance office or career center.

If you have yet to visit your high school's guidance office, now is the perfect time. Guidance counselors are often the first to know about local scholarships in your community, in addition to being very knowledgeable about the financial aid process. You may not even have to make an appointment to see a counselor, as some guidance offices provide bulletin boards dedicated to showcasing local scholarships available throughout the area.

Another approach is to try reaching out to state or local agencies. Nearly every state offers local scholarships that are intended for residents. In some cases, these scholarships may be limited to those attending public colleges or universities, or are only open to students pursuing careers in public service or government. Through state and local agencies, you may also discover scholarship opportunities open to low-income families, minorities, nontraditional students, and students seeking careers in high-demand fields.

## Try Scholarship-Specific Search Engines

Starting your scholarship explorations by searching Google can be quite daunting. In most cases, you'll end up with thousands of search results, and vast majority of them will be completely irrelevant. For this reason, you'll be better off investing your time and energy using a few online scholarship search engines. Here are some sites that can help you narrow your search in finding the most relevant and attainable scholarships.

- CollegeBoard.com
- CollegeNet.com
- CollegeScholarships.org
- Fastweb.com
- ScholarshipMonkey.com

Don't forget to look for state-specific scholarships in your local area.

## Join Member-based Organizations Like NSHSS

In her role as a guidance counselor, Nancy Beane says, "We usually tell the kids not to pay for any kind of scholarship searches. Yet there are a few organizations and societies that can be helpful that do charge a membership fee. The National Honor Society membership dues are usually paid for by your high school principal. The National Society of High School Scholars has individual, lifetime membership dues that help fund the many scholarships, internships, and other opportunities available only to its members. It's almost like belonging to a fraternity, where you pay fraternity dues and you're a member for life. You can always ask about fee waivers. Affiliating yourself with a reputable community of honor students can have benefits beyond your high school graduation."

Joining member-based organizations designed for high achieving students can open a world of possibilities in landing scholarships. Because most of these organizations offer exclusive scholarships only available to members, the chances of winning are dramatically greater.

Members of NSHSS are eligible to apply for exclusive scholarships in the areas of academic excellence, entrepreneurship, leadership, literature, medicine, music, STEM, sustainability, visual arts, and much more. In addition to helping you pay for college, the unique scholarships offered by NSHSS can also help you explore opportunities in studying abroad, getting involved in summer programs, and even attending graduate school.

Landing scholarship money for college and taking the time to submit applications is worth the time and effort. With adequate research, you will learn how to make the overall costs of college far more manageable by earning scholarships, grants, and other forms of financial aid. And by joining member-based organizations you can get a leg up in funding your college education by getting access to exclusive scholarships.

Dr. Susan Thurman, who was the NSHSS Scholarship Director for 16 years, offers up some helpful tips for students applying for scholarships. "Most scholarship applications involve four parts: a resume, an essay, a transcript, and recommendation letters. One of the most important tips to remember throughout the scholarship and college application process is to PROOFREAD everything!"

## Preparing your Resume

Most scholarship applications ask for a resume, and preparing one will also help you keep track of all your accomplishments for your college applications.

Try to keep your resume to one page, starting with your most recent information at the top.

CONTACT INFORMATION: Be sure your contact information is up to date, with address, telephone, email, and current school.

ACADEMICS: Begin with academics: GPA, academic awards, Dean's list, math bowl champion, etc.

LEADERSHIP ACTIVITIES: Officer positions in clubs and organizations, leadership conferences, captain of athletic teams, etc. Leadership doesn't have to mean being the head of a club. Actions, not titles, make leaders.

EXTRA-CURRICULAR ACTIVITIES: Music, sports, clubs/organizations, hobbies, academic camps, employment, internships, part-time jobs, etc.

COMMUNITY SERVICE: Include volunteer activities, including dates

REFERENCES: Include a line that says, References available upon request. If you do wish to include references, be sure to ask for permission from your references and make sure that you have the correct spelling and contact information.

Note: In most cases do not include activities and awards prior to high school (unless you have achieved something truly remarkable, such as winning the National Geography Bee, or founding a charity at a young age).

Here's another sample resume from a "Dream College" Scholarship finalist.

Rimpal Bajwa

### Honors and Awards
Varsity Letters
Key Club (2016 & 2017), HOSA (2016 & 2017), Debate (2016 & 2018), United Way Community Service (2015, 2016 & 2017), Puyallup School District Community Service (2016 & 2017), DECA (2016, 2017 & 2018)

Other Awards
AP Scholar with Distinction, Top 20 Senior in Puyallup High School, Top of Class in Puyallup High School, Top 60 in Original Oratory at National Individual Events Tournament of Champions, Top 50 in Washington State Public Forum Debate, 2-time State Qualifier in Business Law for DECA, National Qualifier in SBE for DECA, National Qualifier for Worlds Debate, Distinction NSDA National Honor Society, 7th Speaker in Public Forum at UNLV, 1st place Corinthian Masonic Lodge Scholarship, 1st place Americans United Essay Contest Winner

### Leadership Activities
NSHSS Ambassador, Key Club President, HOSA Community Service, Debate Captain, Project Committee Treasurer, Vice President FCCLA, National Honor's Society President, Viking Lady Secretary, Key Club Division 30 Activities, Manager of the Viking Blend, March Gladness Student Leadership Council

### Community Service
March Gladness, Communities in Schools, Karshner Elementary School Math Tutor, Khalsa Gurmat School Punjabi and Kirtan Teacher, Gurudwara Singh Sabha, St. Francis House, Step by Step, Puyallup FISH Food Bank, World Vision, Emergency Food Network, Key Club, HOSA, FCCLA, Viking Ladies, National Honor Society

### Extra-curricular activities
Debate, DECA, Concert Band, Puyallup Juniors Volleyball Club

### Work Experience
JCPenney Sales Associate
July 2017- August 2017
Ensure customer satisfaction, process POS purchases, and maintain in-stock and presentable condition assigned areas

Chevron Employee
July 2015 - Present
Responsible for mopping floors, filling ice bags, managing inventory, organizing shelves, and handling hot food

**References upon request**

## You Can Ask for More

Once your acceptance letters and financial aid packages start arriving, you may find yourself in a situation where you are comparing offers and weighing the pros and cons of each choice. If your first choice dream school's financial offer falls short of your needs, you owe it to yourself and the college to reach out and ask for more. There is no guarantee, but even a small boost in aid could tip the scales enough to allow your family to accept. Here is one student's sample letter:

---

RE: Financial Aid Appeal—Knomi Smith

Dear Sir or Madam:

Since my acceptance to Agnes Scott College, I have looked forward to attending in the fall of 2018. Although I have been accepted at other institutions, Agnes Scott is my first choice. This is because Agnes Scott offers greater opportunities for a comprehensive education than some of my other options and lives up to its number 2 ranking of most innovative colleges. I have read about the educational opportunities, travel, partnerships and avenues for hands-on learning there. I have visited the campus and have concluded that Agnes is the best fit for me. I hope to enter the dual degree program and attain degrees in both mathematics and civil engineering. I am convinced by what I know now about Agnes Scott, with its nurturing and uplifting environment, that I will be able to accomplish fully my goals there and enjoy my educational experience.

I thank you for the financial aid and scholarship package that you have granted me. While it enables me to cover most of my costs, my financial situation is such that I feel compelled to request additional funds, if available to me, in order that I may enroll in the fall. I have attached a spreadsheet, which details what has been offered to me by other schools.

My mother is a single parent and is unable to assist me. I have worked hard in high school to overcome educational obstacles and personal hardships. I am eager to attain an education so that I will be able to live more securely than I lived as a young child and also contribute to the well being of others. Therefore, I ask that you reconsider me for further financial assistance. Presently, I need more than [amount offered] to enroll. Anything that you do for me would be greatly appreciated.

Sincerely,

Knomi Smith

Here is another student's story of how he identified and got into his dream school and how he successfully lobbied for more financial aid.

### How I Got Into My Dream School

JAHKORI DOPWELL HALL,
RINGLING COLLEGE OF ART AND DESIGN

When we first enter high school, many times we are not sure about what we want to pursue in the future because the experience is all so new to us. Making new friends, meeting new teachers, learning the ins and outs of our new environment can all seem a bit overwhelming at first. However, for me—my vision never changed, nor did my goal of becoming an artist. In understanding how I got into my dream college, you first would need to understand how I got into my dream high school.

As a child growing up, I was first introduced to art by my cousin. I began to mimic the anime art that she was extremely skilled at. However, as time evolved—I began to develop my own artistic style. When I entered Junior High School, there was an art teacher who encouraged me and I soared from that moment forward. In my eighth-grade year, I remember my mother going with me to just about all the top New York City Art High School's so I could audition for acceptance. When I visited the High School for Art and Design, I immediately knew that it was the school for me and while I put forth my best artwork for all of the schools that I auditioned for, it never mattered about the others because internally I KNEW that I would be going to that High School.

Lo and behold the time came for acceptance decisions, and I was indeed accepted.

My high school experience was amazing! The ninth grade was my exploratory year; however, I did not lose track of my goal. My mother stressed to me the importance of maintaining good grades and attendance and for my twelve years of school, I've never missed a day, and I've maintained honor roll status throughout. By the time I entered 10th grade, I had an idea of where I wanted to go as an artist. Not only did I find passion in painting and drawing, but I also found a love for teaching my art skills to others. In my Sunday school, I was granted an opportunity to co-teach the younger kids and it led me to develop a love for teaching art.

Enter summer at age 16—I joined the Summer Youth Employment Program and I remember my mother telling me that I can select a fast food chain to get introduced to the workforce. I responded immediately stating, "my first job is NOT going to be working in a fast food chain!" There was nothing wrong with working at those places, but I wanted MORE than that. I wanted to teach art, and that was the job that I was looking for. It wasn't long before I was granted my first paid summer job, teaching art to students in grades K-3 at a public school over the summer. I remember everyone (including myself) was in disbelief. As soon as I found out, I told my mom "see, I told you my first job would be teaching." She congratulated me and encouraged me to stick with my instinct and I took that advice to heart.

I joined the drama club in the end of my sophomore year and in addition to artwork, I began acting. After the first two plays, I became actively involved on and off the stage—where I could once again put my artwork to use. I enjoyed acting quite a bit because at home I use to write scripts for me and my five younger siblings to act out. As the year progressed, the focus at home began on college. My aunt dropped off this huge scholarship book and told me to go through it. I had no idea what I was doing, so I kind of put it off to the side figuring I would tackle that in junior year. In the meantime, an afterschool program that my brother was in—invited me to attend several college tours with them since I was closer to being college bound. Now although I appreciated the experience and introduction to college life, I had no interest in attending schools upstate New York.

In the midst of all this, my art work began to get noticed and my art teacher had me sign up for an art program at Studio Institute—Studio in a School. Joining this program gave me recognition that at the time I didn't realize was the beginning of my career expanding into a huge success. In the first year, several of my paintings were selected to be displayed at renowned places such as Scholastic, Lincoln Center, and the famous auction house Christie's. My hard work was starting to pay off and I was proud of the person I was becoming.

That summer, we were in Tampa and while there—my mom scheduled a visit to Ringling College of Art and Design (RCAD). Unfortunately for her, she had to leave Florida to return to work in New York, but she asked my aunt to take me on the tour. This experience was like déjà vu, I immediately fell in love with Ringling College at first sight, but the tour was EVERYTHING. This school had all of the majors that I was interested in pursuing Art/Illustration/Drama/Ceramics, etc. The teachers and staff were so friendly and knowledgeable. I felt at home and thus knew right then that this was where I wanted to go for college. Hence the struggles began....

I couldn't wait to express to my mom how much I loved RCAD. However, my mom advised that I shouldn't put my hopes in just one school in case I am not accepted. I was determined however, and told her that I would be accepted there. I made sure to maintain phenomenal grades and pushed myself to not only obtain silver, but also gold honor roll status consecutively every semester. I was getting into RCAD and NOTHING could change my mind!

As time waits for no one, junior year approached and college discussions, college fairs, and college visits were the main topic at this point in school and at home. The college advisors were constantly on our backs about application deadlines and then I'd get a double dose of that when I went home. The one thing I can say is that my mom was very supportive of my decision for my career path and that made it so much easier for me.

For my senior year, I decided to add a bit more rigor to my schedule, so I enrolled in an Advanced Placement (AP) Art Class and Pre-Calculus to give myself a bit of a challenge. AP Art was amazing, but WHAT WAS I THINKING WITH PRE-CALCULUS???? I enrolled with the expectations that I would have the same teacher I had previously, but when they abruptly changed him, I was almost doomed. I ended up having to get home tutoring which helped me pass the class with a higher grade than I expected, and overall I was glad for the experience and the challenge.

My mom and I visited colleges from the East Coast to the West Coast. At this point, I pretty much narrowed down the five colleges that I was interested in: Ringling College of Art & Design being my number one choice, Rhode Island School of Design, Maryland Institute College of Art, Otis College of Art and Design, and University of Tampa. These schools are amongst the top art schools across the United States and include the majors that I am interested in rather than attending the Ivy League Universities for name status purposes.

The next phase was the application process, and what a process that was! The good thing was that I only had five schools that I was interested in, so there wasn't too much to keep track of. My mom had the deadlines on her calendar, so she sent me reminders and worked with me on getting my paperwork in on time for financial aid.

My school counselors were also very helpful in helping us to get familiar with the process and getting the necessary documents to complete our applications. They provided guidance to me with regards to my college application essay (which I ended up redoing a few times per their recommendations). It was a learning experience, but the good part is that now I can pass on that knowledge I learned to someone else.

Acceptance day finally came around after months of anticipation. I was accepted into all five schools that I applied to and yet again, it was like déjà vu as I stated, "I told you I would get in!" to my mother. I was beyond ecstatic because my dreams were all falling into place. I couldn't wait to reply, to advise Ringling that I was going to accept their offer, but I was instructed to wait until I received all of my financial aid information from the other colleges before I confirmed my enrollment.

I remember some back and forth because everyone (including my AP Art teacher) couldn't understand how I was choosing Ringling College of Art and Design (RCAD) over Rhode Island School of Design (RISD). Everyone was pent up on Rhode Island School of Design because they were a popular school and people knew "the name." Every time I would mention Ringling, people would ask me if I meant the circus. It never fazed me though, because I already knew my capabilities and my plan was to go to Ringling and have such an impact that their name will eventually supersede that of RISD.

Just when you think all is clear and you're on your way, there's always that monkey wrench that is thrown into the equation. My monkey wrench…financial aid! Unfortunately for myself, my parent's income did not qualify me for much student aid, so there were no personal factors that may have tipped the scales in my favor. Though all the financial aid that I received was not much, it was even that much less for Ringling and they had the highest tuition. My mom broke the news to me that they could not afford Ringling college and at that time I remember the pain I felt in my heart.

I had no back up plan because I did not take my counselor's advice on applying to one of the local colleges. My mind was set on going to Ringling so I had no space to accommodate the thought of other colleges in my head. I had to come up with something, some way that I could get financial aid; something had to give because I was NOT going to give up on my dream college. Not when I've come this far in the game.

Alas, another piece of advice I remember hearing my mother say, "A closed mouth won't be fed." I took this advice and decided to open my mouth on paper and pour out my soul to the President of Ringling College expressing how badly I want to attend his school and everything I've done thus far to gain acceptance. I remembered that I had some money saved from my summer job the prior year, so I decided to pay my $500 confirmation fee on my own (knowing there was a possibility that I could forfeit the money if I couldn't go to the school). I wrote a letter to the President of Ringling, with a copy of the letter also going to the VP of Finance & Administration, the Dean of Admissions, the Department Head, Illustration and the Admissions

Counselor. In the letter, I expressed the financial struggle that I now faced in attending the school. I figured it was a long shot, but it was a chance that I would have to take. Lo and behold, a few weeks later I received a letter back from the President as well as a Financial Aid Appeal Letter. The school provided me with some additional funding in order for me to attend. While my mother said it still wasn't enough, she did what she could to work with the additional funding.

Looking back now, the one thing I can say that I would have done differently is spend that first year researching scholarships when my aunt gave me that scholarship book, instead of putting it to the side. Watching how my parents scrambled to get funding together for my first year so that I would not have to take out student loans made me feel a bit guilty about not doing my part to help. I spent useless time on social media that could have been put towards writing scholarship essays. I am trying to make up for it now though by grasping the bit of scholarships that are still circulating out there. I've since been actively applying for various scholarships so my parents won't have to suffer so much of a hardship on my behalf.

The Studio Institute Program that I'm enrolled in recently awarded me with a scholarship for being a committed and active member of their program. They were also recently commissioned by the Neuberger Berman Consulting Firm for some art work in which one of my pieces was selected earning me some additional scholarship money from that firm as well. This year several of my art pieces were awarded a Silver Key and Honorable Mention by Scholastic. Another one of my art pieces was once again selected for display at Christie's auction house in June. I don't know what year 2, 3, or 4 will bring—but I am staying positive and hopeful that something will work out financially as it did for my first-year tuition. The pieces are slowly but surely falling into place and I remain optimistic that as long as I stay focused and continue on the path I'm headed, everything will work out.

As senior year nears its end, I can say that I've found my niche with another part of the drama club besides acting... and that is set design-ing. I was put in charge of the props and designed the stage set for our play on Dracula. I'm grateful for this opportunity as this is going to be helpful when I join RCAD's Improv club. I also plan to start a drama club for other students interested in acting once I become acclimated in the school. I have big ideas for my time at Ringling College. My major will be Illustration with a minor in Art Teacher Education. After college, I plan to get into illustrating/writing children's books while doing commissioned work for a major film studio (i.e. Disney/Pixar/Universal). Ultimately, I plan to rent some office space where I can teach students how to become artists, incorporating all of the things I love into my career.

My advice to getting into your dream college is NEVER give up. When someone discourages you, use that as your motivational push to prove that you CAN do whatever it is you set your mind to. Know that the sky is NOT the limit, but the limit is whatever YOU set it to be—which means you literally are the one who can determine your own success or failure in life. I am your living proof!

Jahkori shared the letter that he wrote to Ringling College of Art & Design to ask for more financial aid.

---

Dear Dr. XXXXXXX:

My name is Jahkori Dopwell Hall and I'm a fourth-year gold honor roll illustration student at the High School of Art & Design in New York City. I am an aspiring artist/art teacher/children's book illustrator whose artwork has been featured for display in Christie's and Lincoln Center. Additionally, my work has also received many awards and recognitions (resume attached).

I've worked very hard at keeping my honor roll status consistent throughout my four years of high school. Before senior year began, I visited well over eight colleges but very few captured my attention. I visited Ringling for the first time in August 2017 and when I returned home, I told my mother that I didn't want to visit any more schools because I AM GOING to Ringling! There were only four colleges that I applied to: Ringling, RISD, MICA and OTIS (in that order). I was accepted to Ringling College, my first choice, which made me extremely happy. The reason I chose Ringling as my first choice was because the campus was not too large and when I visited, I felt very comfortable and at home. While the Ringling College name didn't stand out like RISD, I decided that once I became a student, I was going to make the Ringling College name level up so it could be just as prominent (if not better) than the others.

I've always been taught that sometimes you have to go to the top to seek results, hence we get to the reason I am writing this letter (with the desperate hope that you will be able to help me). I recently received my financial award letter, and despite the scholarships I applied for and the merit awards that I received, my mother said she cannot afford to send me to Ringling and wants me to now look at HCC or USF as alternative options (which I am refusing to do because I've worked very hard maintaining my GPA to get accepted into the top art colleges).

I'm not sure if this matters or can help, but I've been a quarter-year resident of Tampa since 2007 and will be relocating permanently after graduation in June. I've had my Florida permit since I turned 16 and hope to have my license by summer. In the meantime, last year I worked a summer youth employment job and earned $2,100 for the six weeks. I am going to use $500 to reserve my space at Ringling because I want to attend this college ONLY. I understand that there is a chance that I may lose that money, but I always believed in pursuing my dreams and they have never failed me yet. Please don't let this be the first time. My teachers, former summer employers and family can all attest to my dedication, drive and character. I ask that if you can provide a way to help me financially attend your college, you will not regret it!

I look forward to hearing from you soon.

Sincerely,

Jahkori Dopwell Hall

# Making Your Choice

Each student's situation is different. Some of you will have a clear top choice, will be accepted, and have all of the finances worked out. Others may have more than one acceptance package to consider and some soul searching to figure out what school is going to be the best fit. You won't know what your exact options are until all of the offers are on the table. Until then, here are a few student stories that step through their countdown to decision day.

Briana Leone describes her process of narrowing in on her school choice after she did not get into the University of Pennsylvania.

BRIANA LEONE, DREXEL UNIVERSITY
(CRIMINOLOGY AND JUSTICE STUDIES MAJOR)

When the letter arrived in the mail, it was just my sister and I at home. I made her open it as I could not do it myself. Honestly, I do not know why I was that anxious to open a letter from a school that almost did not "make the cut" into my college application process. Perhaps I subconsciously knew better myself than I had realized. When my sister opened the letter and told me I had been accepted, I was more overjoyed than I had expected; especially considering the fact that I had not even remotely thought about Drexel before my decision to apply.

It was the beginning of March when I received my confirmation from Drexel. At the time, I had two possibilities: Drexel or Temple. I was in limbo between the time of my acceptance and spring break. I derailed a little from the ascending prospect of my decision. After all, responses were not required until the beginning of June. What did I do in this interim time? I meditated. I consulted with my parents, my friends, and, after spring break, with my counselor and my English teacher. They all told me it was my decision and no matter which college I chose they would support me. Not at all helpful, let me tell you. I was in a crisis, and the same people who expected me to raise my hand before using the restroom were telling me it was up to me to make the greatest decision of my life. Spectacularly awesome.

For a while I was upset with the adult figures in my life. Why did they expect me to make such a big decision all by myself? I was not prepared at all. Who would be anyway? I was not even an adult yet and they expected me to make a decision that would be able to dictate my life trajectory out of the blue. For the next weeks, as a matter of fact, I decided I would just focus on my IB completion and my senior prom. Conceivably, it may not have been the most mature response to the situation. Actually, it might have been the ultimate childish response. To think about it, I have grown a lot and matured from the 17-year-old high school student I was almost two years ago.

Before I settled the scores with my applications, when I came home one day, I received a packet from Drexel. This packet contained all of the information I needed to know about the school, in addition to something very surprising: I had been awarded a partial scholarship. I was very proud of myself, even surprised to an extent. When my parents came I showed them and I showed my sister. The next day I told everyone who was my friend, as well as my favorite teachers and my college counselor. They all congratulated me, but they asked one thing I was still not sure about: was I going to attend Drexel? I did not answer. How could I decide between Temple, a university I was attached to because of the connections to my mom, and Drexel, an institution that no other family member had attended?

The week I received Drexel's packet, I sat down and weighed my options. On the one side I had Temple, my safe choice. Although I was not awarded a scholarship, it was within my parents' pay range. I definitely did not want to be a financial burden to them. Plus, I considered the Criminal Justice program would be a good alternative to Criminology. Then I asked myself: if every single person in the time of our history had played it safe, would we all be here today with all these commodities at all? The answer was obviously no. I think it was at this point that I truly shifted my prospects to Drexel. They were offering a combined Criminology and Justice Studies program, a decent partial scholarship, and the possibility of gaining experience whilst still being an undergraduate. I weighed these opportunities against those of other institutions and very few institutions in the region offered similar benefits. University of Pennsylvania themselves did not offer such opportunities (for other reasons besides their rejection).

What factors tipped the scales? Firstly, before I decided to move on with my confirmation of attendance to Drexel, I deliberated with my parents again. I wanted to make sure my decision to attend Drexel would not be a financial burden, especially considering I am not the only child in the family. Before I moved forward with my decision, I wanted to secure my parents' approval. After all, they would be (and still are) the ones who support my studies. I felt the need to confirm with them before moving on with my decision. It was not so much my inability to decide, as I have mentioned before; rather, it was my more adult consideration of something greater than myself: my family. Besides, I was not inclined to the prospect of causing a financial burden that, besides stressing my parents, would also harm my sister. I can fend for myself and I want my sister to have the same opportunities I do, which is why the potential of her schooling was factored into my decision.

Truth be told, I thought my parents would tell me attend to Temple, but I also underestimated them. I almost forgot my parents always push to do what I think is best for myself. I underestimated them and that was my fault. Once the four of us talked as a family, I was set on accepting my offer from Drexel. Looking back at my acceptance, I think it was the best thing that happened to me. I am glad various people pushed me to apply to Drexel. Even if it does not work out, I can always do more than what was set for me. My path to and my experiences at Drexel have given me a chance to grow as a person, as well as recognizing that Drexel *is* my dream school, at least for my undergraduate studies. I feel content and satisfied with the path I have chosen thus far. Had I rushed my applications, or had I not even considered Drexel at all, would I be satisfied? Maybe or maybe not. Who knows?

If I had a chance to go back in time, would there be there anything I would change? Truth be told, were I given a chance to go back, I would not change a thing. Probably, the one thing that I would do differently would be to apply for further scholarships; but I managed so far. I believe everything happens for a reason. I see it in this way: had I been accepted into University of Pennsylvania, I would have not gone to Drexel, nor would I have been able to meet Diane, my friend. I would also not have been able to meet Cyndi or Dr. D, my professors, who have been greatly influential in my academic growth thus far. In addition, I believe if I had changed anything in the past, I may not have been able to participate in the course with the people who are present now. Saede, Zoë, and even Gio, are all partners I found here at Drexel. I am satisfied with my acceptance and my course of study, which is why I now consider Drexel my dream school.

You've done the research and spent the hours identifying your best fit options, narrowing your list, applying, getting in, and imagining yourself on the campus of college X, Y, or Z. Making your final choice is the big decision you've been working up to.

KATHLEEN CICERO,
EASTERN MICHIGAN UNIVERSITY

Besides the legwork done in my high school career, I also had to actively search for "the school" itself. At the end of it all, I visited over ten institutions, applied to six, auditioned for the programs at five, pored over numerous scholarships and financial aid packages, did research online, and ruminated countless hours. While this may appear to be an unnecessary amount of work, it was needed for me to at last make my final choice. Before settling on one place, I had narrowed down my options to two schools, which I vacillated between for some time; each had offered me generous scholarships, each had a program in my field of study that would adequately prepare me for my career, and each had a campus that I could see myself being a student at. However, to select the school that was the best fit, I truly had to ask myself where I would feel the most at home. And although I didn't think I would be able to find my preference, my mind kept coming back to one school, where I had immediately connected with the faculty and been impressed by the atmosphere created by the students and staff. That was the college I ultimately chose to attend. The school was Eastern Michigan University.

EMU was not the only school that I considered, however, and not even the first school I looked at. I visited several colleges, beginning my sophomore year, before I even knew what I wanted to study. Even though I did not apply to all the schools I visited, each trip helped me determine what I liked or didn't like in a school, and they sometimes helped "seal the deal" for which schools I decided I did want to pursue. While I was slightly tempted out of curiosity's sake, I did not apply to any Ivy League schools during my college journey, although I did visit the University of Chicago and Northwestern University, which are both very prestigious. I was impressed by and even interested in these institutions, until I learned that they did not offer my area of interest, and therefore, I did not feel they would be the right institutions for me. I did apply to several other schools, including Eastern Michigan University, of course, but also Carthage College, the University of Iowa, Western Michigan University, Illinois State University, and the

University of Indianapolis. Additionally, I auditioned at all of these schools, excluding Western Michigan and Carthage. Truthfully, I was never someone who grew up with a specific school or idea of what a school should be like that was my "ideal" college. I stayed fairly open to all possibilities, and I looked at a wide variety of schools, as shown by the names mentioned. Big, small, in-between, rural, urban, religious-based, liberal-arts focused...I saw them all. Yet, after turning in countless applications and scholarships, going to an array of differing campuses, and completing my auditions, I began to get a sense of where I saw myself in the future. Even if it was done subconsciously, I started to figure out what I was looking for and where I felt the most at home. When I seriously started to consider EMU and take a closer look at it as an option, it began to appeal to me more and more, and I finally came to the conclusion that it was "the school" for me. Although I still looked at other options before eliminating them, I always slightly favored EMU, and it remained my top choice for a large part of my college process.

# A Big Financial Decision

For many, the choice of schools will be heavily influenced by the costs.

AUTUMN SATTERFIELD,
NORTH CAROLINA STATE UNIVERSITY

Overall the application process took many weeks for me because I wanted to highlight myself in the best way possible without repeating what I already had in my application. Each school, generally, has an application fee, which you should know from your spreadsheet. For me, Tennessee was $50, Clemson $70, North Carolina State $85, and Georgia Tech $75. As you can see, it is very expensive to apply to college, so I recommend choosing a few schools. You should have at least one you know you can get into, a few that you can "most likely" get into, and 1-2 that are a "stretch" (whether a big stretch or a small stretch). I would suggest applying early for all of your schools unless it is early decision because it is binding. If you get accepted, you have to go, even if it is not your first pick of schools and even if you get no financial aid. Applying early relieves your stress quickly and many schools only allow you to apply for financial aid if you applied early. I applied early for all of my schools, so I heard back earlier than many of my peers. I first got accepted to Tennessee, then Clemson, followed by Georgia Tech, and finally North Carolina State.

I had my pick of schools at this point. Some of you may have this ability too; others may not. If you are denied acceptance, do not worry about it. It will be heart breaking, but you will still go to college and have a bright future. After you receive all of your admission decisions, you should be receiving your financial aid statements from all schools if you submitted the FASFA on time. Look at how much your tuition is and consider how much money you are receiving. For me, this was the largest factor in my decision on where to go. Georgia Tech gave me the least amount of financial aid and was the second most expensive. In the end, I had to deny myself the opportunity to attend Georgia Tech, and I will instead be arriving at North Carolina State this upcoming August to pursue a dual degree in Chemical Engineering and Paper Science and Engineering. Many of you may have to make this same decision while others of you will be able to attend your dream school.

Looking back on my time in high school and my process of applying for college, I realize I made some mistakes. I should have involved my parents more, and allowed them to help me instead of bearing the burden alone. I think I would also have applied to "harder" schools such as Carnegie Mellon, MIT, and Duke because the future is unknown. I could have been accepted but now I will never know, which is a major regret that I have. I would tell you to not limit yourself. Sometimes you just have to go for it; you may be surprised.

# Revisits for Accepted Students

If you have multiple options and are still not sure which school to choose, a revisit may be the best way to seal the deal.

*NYU had an accepted students weekend called Weekend on the Square where students could come and get a feel of the campus through tours, open houses, club and class events in different buildings. I loved talking to the students and truly appreciated the effort put forward by NYU to make incoming students feel welcome. I also asked friends who attended NYU and were studying the same major that I was interested in. Having received a positive feedback on aspects that mattered most to me further drew me towards NYU. I also liked the fact that NYU followed a semester system rather than trimester or quarter system.*

—Dimple Belani, New York University (NYU)

# Rejected? You Still Have Options

It can sting. The disappointment is real. Allow yourself some time to process the rejection and then lift your chin and explore other options. There are always other options. But don't take my word for it; check out this first-hand advice from your student peers.

*Obviously, I can't guarantee that by following all of these tips you will for sure get into your dream school. That part is entirely between you and the team on the other side of the admissions process (don't worry though; there are actual, real human beings on the other side of your computer screen). You just have to be vulnerably honest in telling your story, and trust that you've done the best work you can do. Even if you don't get accepted to where you thought you wanted to go, you have to believe that you did nothing wrong, and that somehow the universe is guiding you to where you truly belong. I realize that's easier said than done, but that's what happened to me. I applied to fourteen universities and colleges. I was only accepted to five of them. It was devastating because I got almost all of my rejections before I got a single acceptance. However, it is a valuable learning experience and the entire process of application, rejection, and ultimate acceptance helps you to grow as an individual, by forcing you to be reflective about your values and convictions, giving you opportunities (through rejections) to stand firm in your beliefs and to trust the power of your work ethic and any good you've put out into the universe. And when you finally, finally get that magnificent congratulatory letter, it will feel all that much better because you will already know that you deserve to be at the school that will without a doubt become the university of your dreams. So venture forth, be brave, be bold, and above all, be true to yourself and your dreams.*

—MAILE HARRIS, YALE UNIVERSITY

One George Washington University student had his heart set on Stanford after attending a pre-college summer program but ended up not getting in. He writes:

My one piece of advice to students working towards college is to not limit yourself to one university or program. Much of what preparing for college is about is being resilient and open to the notion that not everything will go the way you first intend. Unexpected disappointments, however, are often the source of life's defining moments that make people reconsider who they are and become something all the better for it. People do not know when or how these moments will come their way, but they can be best prepared for them by leaving their options open while sticking to a dream which they can fervently pursue nonetheless. —Treaux Jackson, George Washington University

Being resilient in the face of disappointment and obstacles is a skill that will serve you well for your entire life.

*Just a friendly warning —don't go overboard with all this "dream college" stuff. If you don't get in, no sweat. No matter where you go to college, you can still get a great education and have tons of opportunities to stand out. In fact, attending a less competitive school can even make you stand out more in your classes in the long run.*

—Ali Al Hajaj, Nebraska Wesleyan University

Also try to be optimistic and open to the opportunities that do present themselves—even if they aren't what you, at first, had in mind or things take longer than you expected to work out in your favor.

Phoenix Rose Hoffman,
Laguna College of Art and Design (LCAD)

If I could give you only one piece of advice it would be to keep positive and keep driven. Find that determination inside you and use it as a slingshot to rocket you towards whatever you decided to do after high school. I didn't get into LCAD when I first graduated but I didn't let the rejection stop me. I used it as fuel to drive me to be better next time. I drew everyday, I asked LCAD teachers and students for advice, I focused on building a portfolio that would impress. The second time I applied my counselor at LCAD was astonished by the improvement my art had made over just a few months. She kept assuring me, 'I'm sure you'll get in! You've worked so hard and it really shows!' She even told me she'd encourage the Admissions Judges to accept me because of the rapid growth as an artist and clear ambition I had. Determination and positivity will take you so much farther and make you so much happier than money ever will and you will need it to not only get into a college but also to get scholarships, internships, jobs, etc. Keep your head up, and if at first you don't succeed try again. I was lucky, I found my passion and once I had found it, I used it as a force to keep me moving towards success but it's all right to go to community college and test the waters before you jump off the pier. I am one of the 37.6% of applicants accepted to study animation at LCAD. Laguna College of Art + Design is my dream school, and if I keep driven, keep passionate, keep positive, keep doing all I can to reach my goals I'll be one of a handful of artists who will make an impact.

Through sheer perseverance, you will find a path to success, defined in your own terms.

*In the face of failure, I learned to persevere and overcome my disappointments in search for my dream college, and although the means were rather unconventional by most standards, I still managed to get accepted into my desired college."*

—ABBIGAL MAENG, AUSTIN COLLEGE

## Showing Gratitude

Behind every high school graduate there are an estimated 7,488 loads of laundry, 2,700 loads of dishes, and 19,710 meals. That's a lot of care and feeding. Be grateful.

KATHLEEN CICERO,
EASTERN MICHIGAN UNIVERSITY

No part of my quest to choose a college would have been possible without the guidance of my parents. They were my primary resources and source of comfort. My school counselor was not as heavily involved in my college search and application process, although he was always able to help provide any supplemental materials I needed, such as transcripts, as well as answer any questions I had trouble answering on my own. My parents, on the other hand, were much more active along the whole way, from the very beginnings of my college dabblings up to helping me reach a decision. They offered advice when I began to look at schools, planned numerous college visits and auditions, helped sort through admissions materials, offered additional advice when I truly had reduced my options, and overall provided a support system that was crucial in allowing me to make the most informed choice at the end of April this year. I am so grateful that I had them to make sense of any confusion and simply to know that they were looking out for me.

I'm also grateful to my parents because they pushed me to start doing research and to go on college tours early on. This significantly helped reduce some of my workload later, when I was truly "in the thick" of things, because I had already started to think about my future and college plans. Then, rather than beginning at square one, I could take the next steps to apply and plan visits. I should mention that any pressure I felt was not the result of my parents—they made sure I was on task and being prepared, but always in a positive, motivating way, which is just another reason that they were so instrumental in my college decision-making.

It's easy to be annoyed with your parents and to take them for granted. Right now, while you are in high school, you may feel cramped by their presence; stifled by their rules; skeptical of their ideas; and just generally impatient with them. That's all normal—even expected of teenagers. But in a world where you can be anything…try to be kind.

**Be nice to your parents.** *My parents understood my passion and encouraged me through whatever choice I'd make despite the financial hurdles all students and their families encounter while pursuing a higher education. Sometimes it just takes some space from one another to better understand each other, and college tends to create that opportunity. Keep in touch despite the difference in location or personalities. Listen to their advice; it'll help.*

—PHOENIX ROSE HOFFMAN, LAGUNA COLLEGE OF ART AND DESIGN

There are, no doubt, a whole host of others, besides your parents, who have helped you so far and will continue to offer guidance and support to you en route to the college of your dreams.

*I'm grateful for my counselor and advisor for being such a supportive force in all my struggles, and for the teachers that put up with my time sensitive requests for recommendation letters so late during my senior year. Without them, I might've never gotten where I am now.*

—ABBIGAL MAENG, AUSTIN COLLEGE

Those people who are in your corner, rooting for you, will be just as joyful as you are when you open those acceptance packages and finally decide on the school that will be lucky enough to have you in their freshman class. Be sure to share your good news and openly thank them for being there for you every step of the way.

*Some of the people who helped me through the process were my high school counselors, especially the one who told me to "get on the train" as the opportunity that the university offered me was rare and may not come twice. They also helped me search for scholarships and ways to prepare for college. They were like my parents in school, from when I first arrived there to the moment I left. I thank them for their generosity and help in the entire process. They made copies of the senior class acceptance letters and put them on the wall where people could see—kind of like when mom puts up your drawing on the fridge!*

—STEVEN ESCOBAR-MENDEZ, LEHIGH UNIVERSITY
(FIRST GENERATION HISPANIC STUDENT)

# Advice For Parents

A ny parent's goal is to launch their children into adulthood as confident, responsible, kind, and happy individuals—the same things that students want for themselves! Heading off to college is a major accomplishment towards that goal. There are many steps along the way that can help prepare both parents and students for the transition. It's a process. Some families glide along, no problem. Others struggle with the give and take required as teenagers take on the new responsibilities of the adult world. The following tips are especially designed to help parents turn the controls over to their children, while still being present and supportive in the college application process.

**Be supportive.** Sometimes parents make mistakes about how much guidance they should give. Gently offer your support. Casually suggest your thoughts. Your kids may not listen to you, they may not understand your point of view, or they may be biased toward other priorities. You may think you know what is best, but ultimately your child will need to own the application process and the decision of where they go to college. Somewhere along that thought process your words may stick with them and have meaning, and subtly influence their decisions. Mandates and musts generally don't work well with teenagers.

**Don't do the work for them.** This is a big one. Even if you think your child is falling behind on deadlines or is missing opportunities, this is his or her milestone to meet, not yours. It's his or her life to lead, not yours. The sooner you can give up the control you've had during your child's youth and adolescence, the sooner he will take up the reigns. We need to let our kids fail or at least try some things and stumble in order to be the successes that we want them to be.

**Help your child identify what his or her dream is.** Try to keep your own hopes and dreams for your child to yourself. The following excerpt is all too common:

> In the end, I wound up right where I always wanted to be, even if it was entirely different than what I had initially imagined for myself. Throughout the entirety of my college searches and application process, I spent trying to figure out what I needed to look for in a college that best suited my needs and wants. In my ignorance, I was misled by my parents to believe that only prestigious schools were worth my time, and in light of my misgivings, I kept trying to convince myself that whatever my parents wanted was what I wanted, because after all, parents knew best, right?
>
> —ABBIGAL MAENG, AUSTIN COLLEGE

If you are too concerned with pushing your kids to follow the path that you want for them, versus letting them figure that out for themselves, at some point they will likely be unhappy with the pursuit. They will realize that this is mom and dad's dream for me, not my own.

Here is one student's advice to other students about parental involvement:

*Depending on your circumstance, you may find your parents to be overbearing in the college process. It is important to remind them that ultimately, this is your life and that you need to make the decision that is best for you. However, especially if your parents will be contributing to paying for your college, it is a good idea to listen to their advice and try to implement it.*

—ARIF HARIANAWALA, UNIVERSITY OF TEXAS AT AUSTIN

**Help research schools that align with your child's goals.** Keep in mind as you gather information and visit schools that you and your child should be more concerned about how good of a match a college is for your child than how high its status is. There are a broad range of excellent colleges that offer great educations and the prospect of a successful career. Staying too narrowly focused on a handful of colleges with name recognition and rank is generally not the best or most helpful strategy.

**Set the parameters, advises Nancy Beane.** "Parents have one major responsibility in the college search process and that is to set the parameters, whatever they are—financial, philosophical, geographical, or any other factors that are important to you and your family. Set the parameters for your child and then let go; get out of the way. Don't make the decisions for them. They are the ones going to college, not you." She adds, "I think the last thing you want to be known as is the helicopter parent or the stealth parent. I think the best way to start a huge fight in your family is to insist that your child go to a certain school. If your child hates it, then it's your fault."

**Avoid over coaching.** Admissions representatives warn that applications from students who are "over coached" can be obvious and can hurt admissions chances. It's fine to point out a spelling error on an application or suggest that your child spend more time revising a section, but at the end of the day, the work and achievements need to be the student's. Help your child understand that originality and authenticity are aspects of character that colleges look for and view favorably.

**Watch your We's and You's.** Guidance counselors and college admissions officers tell stories of parents who dominate the conversations meant to be for and led by their children. Let your child ask and answer the questions. And whatever you do, don't say things like "We are applying to…" or "We need to get that GPA up!" If you hear yourself say the word "we" in relation to something your child is responsible for, STOP yourself. Please.

**It's not a family assignment.** No doubt that parents and even siblings will invest some time into supporting a college-bound student. But if the application process starts to feel like a family assignment where you, as a parent, are doing the lion's share of the work to manage the process, it's time to take a step (or two) back. Let your child own the process.

**Encourage dinner table conversations.** Giving your child practice engaging in conversations can help them shine during admissions interviews. Lori Breighner, a global recruitment officer at Duke Kunshan University says, "Preparation for admissions interviews shouldn't be something families consider only immediately before they are scheduled. The student that performs best in an admissions interview will be one that is comfortable meeting new people and has experience speaking with adults in different settings and on different levels." She adds, "An admissions interview, at its core, is simply a *conversation*. Parents can help their students cultivate these all-important 'people skills' by initiating meaningful conversations as often as possible. Any discussion—at the dinner table, on the way to soccer practice, even texts back and forth—can serve as an opportunity to model the kind of discussion that a student should able to sustain with their interviewer. By regularly posing open-ended questions, challenging ideas, drawing out opinions, and asking them to expand on key points, parents can help their students learn how not only to *impress* their interviewer but *engage* them in thoughtful discourse."

**It's not a race to the finish line.** If your child is slow to get his or her head in the college application game, it's OK. Try to honor where he or she is and know that not everyone has to follow the same script and strict timeline that the system prescribes. College is too important and too expensive a step to rush into if your child is not ready. Let your child know that a gap semester or year to work, go to community college, or explore other options can be a smart idea.

**Encourage a healthy balance of academics, athletics, extracurriculars, and leisure time.** Even the most advanced students may be better off pursuing unstructured activities that foster intellectual curiosity and keep the joy in learning. Overloading on AP courses or pushing too hard on the soccer field can lead to burn-out and undue stress. In the end, you want your child to find a healthy balance that is manageable and sustainable. Too much pressure from parents can backfire. Yet one single mom whose seven children all received scholarships to attend college advises parents to "keep your children involved in positive activities because if you don't, someone else will present something negative to fill the void."

**Take comfort in the student stories shared in this book.** Reading the many different kinds of journeys and alternative paths to success will hopefully make it easier for your child to imagine and realize his or her own successful journey. Feel good about the journey, no matter what direction it leads.

## Top 10 Pieces Advice for Parents: (Parent to Parent)

Michael Koenig, a parent and High School Guidance Counselor at Proctor Academy in New Hampshire, has guided his own children and thousands of high school students and their parents through the college application process. He shares his top 10 pieces of advice.

1.  Trust your child enough to allow them to make mistakes—Step back and see them as emerging adults.
2.  Let your child know you are there to help, not control– Listen more than talk to your child.
3.  Try to guide, not push—It's about the soft sell.
4.  Do not do for your child what they are capable of doing for themselves— Empower, do not enable.
5.  Resist living vicariously through your student—You've been there, it's your kids' time!
6.  Be prepared for frustration, disappointment, learning, and surprises—This makes you feel like a parent!
7.  Understand there is no such thing as "One Perfect College." There are hundreds of amazing colleges and universities.
8.  What you discover is often better than what you plan—We all love surprises!
9.  Don't fall for hype or follow the crowd—Advise your child to follow his or her heart!
10. Allow this process to be an educational one, filled with discovery, excitement, and growth.

What do your kids want you to know? According to the Student Affairs office at Temple University, these two statements encapsulate the most common things that students wish their parents would understand:

*"Struggle is OK. Don't always tell me that everything is going to be fine."*

*AND*

*"Let me figure out what my plans are going to be, even if they need to change."*

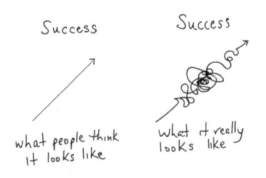

# Congratulations!

That "Congratulations!" email, text, or letter is what you are working so hard to achieve. It will come. Trust in yourself and know that you will find a great school that is just as happy to have you on campus, as you are to attend. If you have learned anything from the expert advice and first-person stories of the students in this book, I hope it is that there is no one way to identify and get into the college of your dreams. Everyone's story is different and yours will be too. How you get from here to there is up to you and your particular set of circumstances.

When you look at others' achievements, it is easy to think that their path to success was a straight line. The reality looks a lot different.

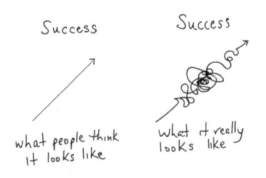

All of that hard work, those detours, and those confusing and sometimes painful setbacks are all part of the process of formulating your dream and writing your own story. Be sure to celebrate the small measures that bring you closer to your goals. Try not to let the struggles derail your dreams for long.

> *Dreams are what make us who we are. They define our aspirations, make us hopeful for the future, and inspire us to keep striving for better. Though we often plan out exactly how to make our dreams come true, the day we actually see our fantasies become reality is surprising, unbelievable, and wonderful beyond all imagining. When one spends so many years dreaming and hoping and working toward a goal, the day one sees it come true is unfathomably marvelous.*

—MAILE HARRIS, YALE UNIVERSITY

Figuring out where you will go to college probably feels like a monumental hurdle right now, but you will find your academic home after high school.

> *So here is my advice: don't worry so much about where you go to school. Maybe it's an Ivy League and maybe it's a community college. No matter where you end up going, you will come to love your school. You will meet people who are just like you and who are drastically different from you. But you will all struggle with the same type of math and essays and will bond through that struggle. You will have school spirit and pride because it's hard not to when you spend so much of your time on one campus. No matter what school you attend, you can be whatever type of student you want to be. I recommend being the kind of student who takes advantage of the opportunity to go to college, because most of us only get to experience that one time. Learn every single possible thing you can, talk to every person you have the chance to, join some clubs or sports or groups, and try everything once.*

> *And when you graduate, you find that no one cares if you were number 1 or number 100 in your high school class or whether your sat score was 1600 or 1200 or how many extracurriculars you have on your resume. And for the most part, no one cares where you went to school. They will care about what kind of person you are, what kind of knowledge and skills you offer, and what you can contribute to the world.*

—JASMINE AL-AIDY, GEORGIA TECH

# Advice from Claes Nobel

I will leave you with this guiding advice from Claes Nobel, the senior member of the family that established the Nobel Prizes, which are recognized worldwide as the most prestigious awards available in the fields of literature, medicine, physics, chemistry, economics and activism for peace. Mr. Nobel knows the importance of setting goals and working diligently to achieve them.

**Keep Your Eye On the Prize.** If acceptance to the college of your dreams is your prize, keep it in mind often. Let images of you at that college replay in your brain like a recurring dream. That dream will be more vivid once you visit schools, but your imagination can run free until you have that chance. The important thing is to have a goal—an ideal—to strive for and to keep you on track.

Remember that goal when you bump up against tough times or find yourself with a choice between doing just enough to get by and making the extra effort to excel. Why? Because you have to work really hard and stay focused to earn big prizes. The Nobel Prize takes a lifetime of passion and hard work to earn. You can earn your prize in just four years of hard work in high school. And who knows, once you graduate from your dream school and apply your degree in a meaningful career, you might just be one of the select few to be awarded a Nobel Prize. Go for it!

**Celebrate Our Good Earth!** In the grand scheme of life, the good earth is our most cherished prize. I like to greet people by saying, "Good Earth!" Say it now. Out loud! GOOD EARTH! It feels good. Those positive feelings (caused by endorphins) can help you do great things.

**Learn. Lead. Change the World.** I believe that the human race can be fundamentally better than it is, and students like you will be the ones to change the world to make it what it can be. You are the most formidable proponents of change.

**Honor What Is Most Important in Your Life.** Ask yourself what is truly important and stay true to your beliefs, intuition, and good sense. I believe we should all aspire to uphold these few ideas as important and necessary:

- Cultivate Universal Peace and Earth Ethics
- Your time on Earth is a loan. Use it well!
- In your cool heads, warm hearts and strong, caring hands rests the world's finest and best hope for the dignified survival of Earth and humanity. Be the movers and the shakers and the framers of The New World!
- **Be Civilized.** Treat each other with respect, have good manners, and behave with civility.

**Practice the Seven Rights.** You have the ability to embody all that is right with the world by following these seven tenets.

1. **Right Thought.** Your mind is a dynamic "Master Builder." It creates reality! Dream lofty dreams! Thoughts materialize! Everything in our universe, in the world, in the room where you sit...yes, even each and every person reading this book all originated first in thought. Just think about that!

2. **Right Words.** Words are most powerful. Once a word leaves your mouth, not even the strength of 10,000 elephants can pull it back again.

3. **Right Deed.** Stop talking...start walking! Let love, dignity, honor, and truth be the noble hallmarks of your character.

4. **Right Attitude.** Show Gratitude! Be patient! Smile, laugh and be kind, positive, and helpful to all. Practice True Love Be a good listener! Listen with your HEART!

5. **Right Livelihood.** Step lightly on the Earth! Leave no footprints!

6. **Right Here.** You do not have to go to the faraway corners of the world. Start world transformation and world betterment in your own community. Start digging in your own backyard. Dig deep! You might find diamonds!

7. **Right Now.** Do not procrastinate! No more excuses like you have no time or you do not care. Become an active and very busy person for world betterment and world change.

# Acknowledgments

A heartfelt thank you to all of the students who contributed their wisdom and honest accounts of their college application process by submitting stories and essays. Most of the students quoted in the book were winners, finalists, semi-finalists, or participants of the NSHSS "How I Got Into My Dream College" Scholarship.

| | |
|---|---|
| Eyram Akakpo | University of Akron |
| Jasmine Al-Aidy | Georgia Institute of Technology |
| Cassandra Allen | Wellesley College |
| Rimpal Bajwa | Georgetown University |
| Lanae Barrow | Bowling Green State University |
| Esther Bedoyan | Carnegie Mellon University |
| Dimple Belani | New York University |
| Selah Bell | Yale University |
| Kayla Campbell | The Ohio State University |
| Lauren Campbell | University of California, Los Angeles |
| Jaron Chalier | Carleton University |
| Christian Chambers | Hampton University |
| Natalie Chandler | Baylor University |
| Kathleen Cicero | Eastern Michigan University |
| Lauryn Darden | New York University |
| Tejna Dasari | The University of Texas at Austin |
| Dominique Dempsey | American University |
| Garrison Funk | Bard College at Simon's Rock |
| Soleil Gaylord | Dartmouth College |
| Eduardo Gonzalez | University of Chicago |
| Bethany Greenwood | Florida State University |

| | |
|---|---|
| Jahkori Dopwell Hall | Ringling College of Art and Design |
| Ali Al Hajaj | Nebraska Wesleyan |
| Arif Harianawala | The University of Texas at Austin |
| Maile Harris | Yale University |
| Phoenix Hoffman | Laguna College of Art and Design |
| Christopher Kim | United States Naval Academy |
| Briana Leone | Drexel University |
| Abbigal Maeng | Austin College |
| Steven Escobar-Mendez | Lehigh University |
| Felix Morales | Florida Institute of Technology |
| Sydney Price | Spelman College |
| Kevin Qualls | Brown University |
| Gillian Rabin | Oglethorpe University |
| Bailey Rasic | Fashion Institute of Design and Merchandising |
| Jaquez Robinson | American Musical Dramatic Academy |
| Ellie Rostan | Bard College at Simon's Rock |
| Kelsey Santiago | University of Florida |
| Autumn Satterfield | North Carolina State University |
| Elise Schlecht | Barnard College |
| Shanaya Sidhu | University of California, Los Angeles |
| Alison Sin | Cornell University |
| Knomi Smith | Agnes Scott College |
| Nicholas Wright | New York University |

I would also like to thank the team at NSHSS for their research, editing, and production support, especially Dr. Susan Thurman, Grace Dent, Brandi Patterson, and Lee Lewis.

I learned so much from the many college admissions representatives, high school guidance counselors, and industry experts who offered their advice and counsel during the writing of this book. Friends and colleagues, you are wise and wonderful. Thank you!

I am forever grateful for the ongoing support and input from Claes Nobel, who not only contributed his wisdom to the book but also stands strong in support of me and my work. I would also like to acknowledge and thank those individuals who have inspired me along my journey. Dr. Henry Stanford, who served as president of five colleges and universities, including the University of Miami and the University of Georgia; Dr. Di Yerbury, first woman to be selected as a university vice-chancellor (president) of an Australian university, Macquarie University; Dr. John DiBaggio, former president of Michigan State University and Tufts University; Dr. Judith Kuipers, former chancellor of University of Wisconsin, La Crosse and president emerita of Fielding Graduate University; Ambassador Andrew Young; Todd Corley, chair of the NSHSS Foundation; Dr. Bernice King, CEO of the King Center; Johnnetta Cole, former president of Spelman College and former director of Smithsonian Institution's Museum of African Art; and Dr. Larry Schall, president of Oglethorpe University.

I would also like to thank Nancy Beane, former president of the National Association for College Admissions Counselors (NACAC), for all of her years of support, and all of the members of NACAC for all they do to benefit young students in their pursuits of excellence.

Thank you to my readers and all who purchase this book—a portion of the profits will fund scholarships that help additional students go to college and live their dream.

# Resources

Many of the resources mentioned in the book are listed here, along with a few extras.

## College Search Tools and Advice

BigFuture.CollegeBoard.org

Coalition for Colleges http://www.coalitionforcollegeaccess.org

CollegeConfidential.com

CollegeFactual.com

CollegePoint.info (free college advisors for qualifying students funded by Bloomberg Philanthropies)

College Scorecard (US Dept. of Education) https://collegescorecard.ed.gov

Fiske Guide to Colleges https://www.sourcebooks.com/fiske-guide-to-colleges.html

MyOptions.org (from NRCCUA and ACT)

Niche.com

Quora.com

US News & World Report

Washington Monthly https://washingtonmonthly.com/2018college-guide

## Essay and Personal Statement Resources

PROMPT.com

*"The 4 Most Common Essay Mistakes and How to Fix Them"*

TheCollegeEssayGuy.com

*"Conquering the college admission essay in 10 steps"* By Alan Gelb

## Financial Aid

FAFSA deadlines can be found on fafsa.edu.gov

"Focus on the Net Price Not the Sticker Price" by CollegeBoard BigFuture

## Gap Year

AFS

College Edge (from Columbia University)

EF Gap Year

Gap Year Association

Global Volunteers

Outward Bound

Rustic Pathways

Where There Be Dragons

## Scholarship Search Tools

CollegeBoard.com

CollegeNet.com

CollegeScholarships.org

Fastweb.com

NSHSS.org (Scholarships and opportunities available to members in high school, college and beyond. Visit www.nshss.org/scholarships for scholarship descriptions, details and deadlines. Visit www.nshssfoundation.org for scholarships through the NSHSS Foundation.)

ScholarshipMonkey.com

## Standardized Tests

ACT Academy — Free test prep at academy.act.org

Khan Academy

Princeton Review

SAT: Understanding Scores https://collegereadiness.collegeboard.org/pdf/understanding-sat-scores.pdf

TestMasters https://www.testmasters.net

## For Parents

"How to Raise an Adult: Break Free of the Overparenting Trap and Prepare Your Kid for Success" by Julie Lythcott-Haims

"Getting In" by Malcolm Gladwell

NPR: "Applying to College or Know Someone Who Is? Here's How to Build a List"

"Making Caring Common Project" by the Harvard Graduate School of Education

# About the Author

James W. Lewis is President of the National Society of High School Scholars (NSHSS), which he established in 2002 along with friend and co-founder, Claes Nobel, senior member of the family that established the Nobel Prizes.

NSHSS supports more than 1.6 million lifetime members, ages 15 to 32, from 170 countries and is recognized as the world's largest honor society for young high achievers. As the president of NSHSS, James is a mentor for high school students from freshmen to seniors and to college students making the transition to their career. NSHSS is designed to recognize diverse students and encourage them to be a positive influence through service, leadership, and volunteer programs.

In 2015, James was named a Top 10 Diversity Champion by The Global Diversity List, published and supported by *The Economist*. James's vision for diversity and inclusion and international education is reflected in NSHSS's partnerships with world-class educational and leadership programs from around the globe. NSHSS has university partners that provide scholarships, host member events, and offer academic and leadership programs to NSHSS members. The Society also partners with many outstanding companies. His constant pursuit of more opportunities for minority and underrepresented students led him to establish the NSHSS Foundation, which offers donor-directed scholarships and also focuses on STEM (Science, Technology, Engineering, and Mathematics), Business, Finance, and Public Policy. Organizations James has founded have awarded over $20 million in student scholarships.

James was the youngest recipient of the American Eagle Award from the Invest In America National Council presented in the U.S. Senate. This award is bestowed upon recipients who exemplify outstanding leadership and make significant contributions to the American free enterprise system. Other recipients include President Ronald Reagan, Malcolm Forbes and former Chief Justice of the Supreme Court, Warren Berger.

James was a two-term board member of the Georgia Society of Association Executives (GSAE), a professional association of non-profit and trade organizations and associations, as well as a trustee on the GSAE Foundation Board.

Selected as an Olympic Torch Bearer in 2002, James carried the Olympic flame through the Atlanta neighborhoods surrounding the Martin Luther King Memorial. He currently serves on the Advisory Board for "be a STAR" (Show Tolerance and Respect), an anti-bullying campaign created by The Creative Coalition. The Creative Coalition educates and mobilizes leaders in the arts and entertainment industry with organizations like NSHSS on issues of social importance.

In 2012, Atlanta Mayor Kasim Reed of Atlanta bestowed the city's top honor on James, The Phoenix Award, in appreciation for his outstanding contributions to the City of Atlanta and its citizens. "Atlanta is truly blessed to say James W. Lewis is one of her own. He gives so much to students and works hard alongside of them to set an example for others to give selflessly," stated Mayor Reed.

Also in 2012, James was awarded the Champions Awards at the World Diversity Leadership Summit. Nearly 400 senior global executives from over 150 of the world's leading corporations were a part of the international summit. James received this award for his passion of opening doors and opportunities for young leaders from around the world. Concerning this honor and award, Todd Corley, chief diversity & inclusion officer at OhioHealth, says "James's personal commitment to diversity leadership is unparalleled and is evidenced in his life's work to provide students with resources to excel academically and professionally."

At Georgia State University (GSU), James earned his Bachelor's in Business Administration (B.B.A.) degree followed by a Master's Degree in Public Administration (M.P.A.). He taught at GSU's Andrew Young School of Public Policy at the graduate level for many years. He was also the commencement speaker for GSU in the year 2000. James was recently selected as a University Trustee at Oglethorpe University.

The mark of a true visionary is not in the projects he creates; it is in the benefits that others reap moving mankind forward. James W. Lewis has set the bar in empowering youth in the world of scholarship, academics, diversity, inclusion, international education, and volunteerism with his programs, leadership, and genuine care for humanity.

CPSIA information can be obtained
at www.ICGtesting.com
Printed in the USA
FSHW021525300719